Critical Acclaim for Jerry R. Wilson's
Word-of-Mouth Marketing:

"This action-oriented book relies on how-to, not theory. Writing in plain language and using stories, humor, and easy-to-understand diagrams, Wilson shows how businesses can harness and direct the powerful force of word-of-mouth marketing."

Booklist

"Every entrepreneur understands an effective marketing program is necessary . . . and expensive. . . . Jerry R. Wilson shows how to market your business for free by providing great service and spreading your business's reputation by word-of-mouth."

Entrepreneur

WORD-OF-MOUTH MARKETING

Jerry R. Wilson

JOHN WILEY & SONS, INC.

New York • Chichester • Brisbane • Toronto • Singapore

This text is printed on acid-free paper.

Copyright © 1991, 1994 by Jerry R. Wilson

Published by John Wiley & Sons, Inc.

Library of Congress Cataloging in Publication Data:

Wilson, Jerry R.
  Word-of-mouth marketing / by Jerry R. Wilson
    p. cm.
  Includes bibliographical references.
  ISBN 0-471-52495-6 (cloth)   ISBN 0-471-00858-3 (paper)
  1. Customer service—United States—Public opinion. 2. Customer
satisfaction—United States. 3. Customer behavior—United States.
4. Advertising—United States. 5. Public opinion—United States.
I. Title.
HF5415.5.W59   1991   90-39271
658.8'12—dc20

Printed in the United States of America

10 9 8 7 6 5 4 3 2

Dedication

To Dad and Mom, Roy and Ruth Wilson, who unknowingly introduced me to the basic principles of word-of-mouth marketing. They truly lived these rules in their business and personal lives, and witnessing the payoff encouraged me to explore their lessons in more depth.

To my wife Sherrie, who put up with my passion for research, helped with the book, and supported me in everything I've ever done. She has truly exceeded my expectations. And to Doug, Brian, and Angela, three kids who make me proud to be a father.

Preface

You say you don't advertise? *Wrong!*

You advertise in a thousand different ways in the hundreds of transactions you conduct every day. What you do and how well you do it either generates talk about you and your organization, or it doesn't. This results in positive advertising, neutral advertising, or negative advertising—in the form of word of mouth. And, as you're about to discover, word of mouth is the most powerful advertising of all.

Consultant Bob Levoy says, "The proof of the pudding is not in the tasting but in whether people return for a second helping." Failure to grasp that simple wisdom is one of the reasons most new businesses fail within five years. The majority of those who do survive still wallow in mediocrity. They make enough sales and profits to keep their doors open, yet fail to achieve the growth and momentum to become legendary.

To understand why so many businesses fail to succeed, you must understand the awesome power of word-of-mouth marketing. While

American businesses are the best in the world at getting the first sale, the awful truth is that they are horrible at getting customers and clients to take that second taste; to buy a second time.

We know how to do slick direct mail campaigns, television spots, and radio commercials. We choose expensive locations, spends millions on atmosphere and ambience, and yet fail to capture the customers' attention so they are motivated to buy again. Why? I suggest that the cause is negative word of mouth. Helping you to overcome that problem is the purpose of this book. On the other hand, if you motivate buyers to talk positively about you, you also win the word-of-mouth referral factor—the most powerful and profitable marketing tool available today.

As you read this book keep these thoughts in mind:

Word of mouth is rarely based on one thing you do . . . or don't do. Instead, it's the result of hundreds of little things you consistently do a little bit better than your competition.

Success at a pro-active word-of-mouth campaign requires a "top-down" obsession with managing what people are saying about you. Everyone in your organization must listen to *everyone*, from customers to employees, from suppliers to your landlord, from stockbrokers to the custodian.

Word-of-mouth marketing is not limited to businesses. Just as the butcher, baker, and candlestick maker can profit from these strategies, so can pastors, volunteer leaders, executive directors, and fund raisers. Businesses and organizations, both large and small, can use the tools of word-of-mouth marketing.

You may need to substitute your unique term for what we frequently refer to as customers. Doctors call them patients, attorneys call them clients, hotels call them guests, and associations call them members. For the purpose of this book, we'll call them customers.

Word-of-mouth marketing is not intended to replace the things you currently do well. Instead, use it to supplement and enhance your current efforts in all the other areas.

There is an order to word-of-mouth marketing. When you use the strategies in this book to capitalize on that order, what you will have is a word-of-mouth marketing plan that can supplement an existing marketing plan.

Most of all, remember that word of mouth can be managed. You are not merely at the mercy of those who talk. You can take control and use these ideas to put together your own word-of-mouth marketing program. What are we waiting for? Let's get going!

JERRY R. WILSON

Indianapolis, Indiana

For a live interpretation of the principles of word-of-mouth marketing at a convention, conference or sales meeting, call Jerry Wilson at 1 (800) 428-5666 or (317) 257-6876; or write to Jerry Wilson and Associates, 5335 N. Tacoma Avenue, Suite 1, P.O. Box 55182, Indianapolis, IN 46205.

Acknowledgments

Many people have helped me with *Word-of-Mouth Marketing*. If I've learned just one thing from writing it, it's that I could not have done it alone.

My very special thanks go to James V. Smith, Jr. Without his tireless efforts as sounding board and researcher this book would probably have remained only a dream. You will hear more about Jim, a truly gifted organizer and writer.

Long before I could prove these principles would work, Dave Ellison trusted me to spend money we didn't have to try ideas I couldn't prove would work in our stores. Special thanks also go to Roger, Jim, Harry, Mike, Mae, and Larry for putting up with me while I tried to do everything a little better.

To Cindy Elliott, our National Coordinator, who willingly handled hundreds of tasks, from manuscript to mailings, with professionalism and dedication. Her help is appreciated.

To George Spelman of Murray Corporation and Mark Saunders of MCI Communications, who helped me sort out the principles of word-of-mouth marketing. Their testing in the real world validated that the ideas work, and their friendship is a real treasure.

To Jeff Herman, our agent, who believed in the book and handled details with the publisher, and to Gwen Jones at John Wiley & Sons, for making it a pleasure to work through tons of details, go my sincere compliments.

Finally, to the thousands who have read my articles, hired me as a speaker, attended my seminars, or purchased our products, I want you to know your support was appreciated. Your ongoing input, feedback, and support are what keep me going.

Contents

SECTION *I*

The Dynamics of the Talk Factor

> **"You can be just as organized, thoughtful, and systematic about 'word-of-mouth advertising' as about media buys."**
>
> **—Tom Peters in *Thriving on Chaos***

1

What Word-of-Mouth Marketing Is and What It Can Do for You

The *talk factor* is a term I coined to describe the dynamics of word of mouth, but it's a concept you're completely familiar with in practice. I'll bet I could name a dozen cases where you have lived the *talk factor*. Let me describe one of your most common experiences, the dining experience. I know you'll remember it because of what Samuel Johnson said: "A man seldom thinks with more earnestness of anything than he does his dinner."

You've just finished eating at the Hungry Heifer Restaurant where the food hasn't been bad, but the service has been slow. The waiter has had to be reminded to bring your side order, and you had to use your napkin to wipe water spots off the silverware. It hasn't been really terrible, but you've had a bad day, so instead of enjoying the dining out experience, you get annoyed. The waiter brings your check and asks, "Has everything been all right?" You say, "Fine." Outside, walking to your car, you turn to your spouse and grumble, "We're never going back to that place." The next day, one of your friends says, "I'm looking for a good place to take my friend for dinner—anybody have a suggestion?" You say, "Yes, if you're looking for a *good* place, stay away from the Hungry Heifer. I had dinner there last night. The food's not bad, but the service was one little disaster after another." Your friend says, "Glad you told me that before we wasted our money. We've always gone to Charlie's. The food's great and the service is consistent. We'll probably go back there." Your friend turns back to work putting screws in screen doors on the assembly line. A third party says, "Heard about that new restaurant, the Hungry Heifer?" The friend says, "Yes. I hear bad things about it. In fact, the joint is terrible. Don't go unless you want ptomaine poisoning!" The third party later goes to the barber shop, where the conversation turns to the Hungry Heifer. "The health department ought to shut the place down," says the third party. "I hear a couple of people nearly died of food poisoning." Later, you see the place *has* shut down. The reason? Competition? Location? Maybe. But I always wonder just how much can be attributed to negative word of mouth.

Although the story is obviously fictional, I'm positive you have experienced something like it. In a nutshell, it's a portrayal of the *talk factor* dynamics that make up what is commonly called word of mouth. This book focuses a microscope on the *talk factor* and word of mouth. The larger point of this story is that word of mouth is eating up thousands of organizations across America, one bite at a time—and the people inside don't even know what's happening until it's too late. If you're the owner of your own Hungry Heifer—or a department manager in a company, or a volunteer coordinator, or even a pastor of a congregation—you'll want to know the strategies that put word of mouth to work *for* you instead of *against* you.

You could trace the history of word of mouth back to the Bible's creation story, when the serpent tempted Eve to sample the forbidden fruit. Then Eve talked Adam into the same offense, whereupon they wore out their welcome in Paradise. Just look at the burdensome reputation snakes have had to live and die with since that story was first told! Since that time, talk has been recognized as a factor in every human endeavor. In business, a term evolved to refer to talk as a factor in spreading a company's reputation—word of mouth.

Word of mouth. Everybody talks about it, but nobody ever does anything about it. That's because almost nobody believes anything *can* be done. People in businesses, practices, organizations, congregations, classrooms, and professions believe they are as powerless to change word of mouth as to change the weather.

But you *can* do something about word of mouth. You *can* make it a part of your overall marketing plan. You *can* learn how the *talk factor* works. You *can* use what you learn in the day-to-day building of your company reputation. And you can even launch a word-of-mouth marketing blitz to introduce new products, ideas, and campaigns.

This book examines the dynamics of word-of-mouth marketing and shares the findings with you (the first finding is that word-of-mouth marketing principles are both powerful and distinctive). This book can help you use the many other findings to advance your organization's business goals. Word-of-mouth marketing can become a powerful management tool in achieving your overall strategic plan.

That's what this book can do for you.

Now, let's get on with it. First let's deal with the *you*. Who are *you?*

Who Should Learn about Word-of-Mouth Marketing

- Owners, managers, executives or leaders in corporations, government agencies, and non-profit organizations *of any size*
- Professionals—accountants, dentists, doctors, lawyers
- Volunteers, directors, entrepreneurs, military officers, government service civilians
- Association executives, club officers, youth athletic coaches
- Consultants, teachers, pastors—leaders of any kind of group

■ Any employee or group member who wants an organized program of self-advancement in his or her career and personal life

A Word-of-Mouth Marketing Quiz

1. How many people did not—repeat, did *not*—come to your place of business today?

2. How many dollars worth of business did you not do yesterday because people are avoiding you because of the word of mouth on your service?

3. How many of your employees just yesterday were badmouthing your organization to potential clients, patients, or customers?

4. How many people drove by your place of business yesterday, not because of your product or price, but because of your service or attitudes to be found inside your doors?

5. How many people voted against you with their feet and hands yesterday because of what they have heard about you? (They voted with their feet by going into a different store. They voted with their hands by dialing a phone number other than yours.)

6. Finally, ask yourself this all-important question: What would happen to your organization if everybody had an *alternative* to doing business with you?

You don't have the precise answers to these questions. If you did, it would be frightening. Or would it? Maybe the answers, however frightening, would awaken you to the negative image you are generating about yourself through word of mouth. As you read on, looking for benefits, keep in mind that last question: What would happen to your organization if everybody had an *alternative* to doing business with you?

Specific Benefits in This Book

■ You will find a thorough discussion of the dynamics of the *talk factor* and a unique new marketing tool, the word-of-mouth marketing pyramid.

■ You will learn why every employee or member of your organization must become familiar with the power of word of mouth and must learn how to use it to the company's benefit.

■ You will discover an organized, systematic, pro-active program for capitalizing on the power of word of mouth.

■ You will learn the strategies for managing talk as a productive marketing, promotional, or public relations tool.

■ You will find new techniques for running different campaigns:
  • Long- or short-term campaigns
  • Deliberately planned campaigns
  • Ad-hoc campaigns
  • Emergency damage control campaigns
  • Political campaigns, fund-raisers, product launchings, or image changers

■ You will see how to put word-of-mouth marketing principles to work in every aspect of business management from customer service to sales, advertising, product development, and personnel management.

You're going to like two features of this book in particular—one, it's action oriented, and two, it's written in plain language. The book relies on how-to, not theory. It's a direct, non-academic narrative using stories, humor, and easy-to-understand diagrams. You don't need an MBA to understand and use word-of-mouth marketing.

Finally, the book is intended for companies and organizations of any size. Yes, the Fortune 500 businesses have paved the way as case studies for the excellence and customer service books. Many examples in these pages come from small- to medium-sized companies. The ideas can be put into action by any of the non-giant "Fortune 10 million" companies in America.

How This Book Is Organized

Section I. The Dynamics of Talk in Word-of-Mouth Marketing

Figure 1 tells the story of Section I. Most companies fail to address a systematic word-of-mouth marketing effort in their overall marketing

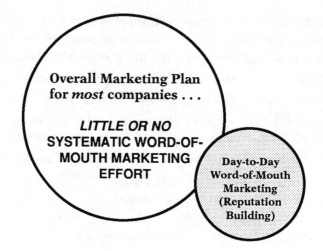

Figure 1

plan. If they prepare a formal marketing plan at all, word of mouth is incidental to it.

But like it or not, every company does have a reputation or image. And every day, people talk about the company, its products, and its services. This talk adds a little or subtracts a little from that reputation. Day by day, a hidden, spontaneous, unsystematic network of talk is either eroding or building the company image.

Here's a true story that illustrates how all the forces of word of mouth might be operating at the same time, pushing and pulling for and against a company image. I piled three other executives into my car to take them to lunch. My idea was to go to a reliable neighborhood steak house that had never disappointed me. "No way, José," responded Executive Number 1. "The salad bar's always empty and nobody seems to care." Just like that, the restaurant lost at least $40 worth of business. Number 2 had never been there, so the first word he heard about it was negative. Number 3 piped up to say, "You know, it surprises me to hear you say that. I've eaten there a lot and never been disappointed—but I never have the salad bar, so you may be right about that part of it."

Do you see how word of mouth operates unsystematically if left to its own devices? Chances are, the day-to-day effects of word-of-mouth marketing efforts can be described in the same terms as this more or less chaotic scene in my car. All the ingredients are there, operating invisibly —for better or for worse—on your business. Could anything have been done to crystallize a unanimous opinion from the four of us? Yes. And those are the strategies we discuss in the book. But for now, just realize how random word of mouth can operate.

Section I describes the elements of word of mouth so you can begin to understand how to make sense of them. Here are the main principles examined:

- The *talk factor* is a term that describes the qualities and dynamics of talk.
  - Talk is not a passive, uncontrollable, amorphous intangible, but a measurable, collectible, manageable commodity that can move results to the bottom line like any other marketing tool.
- Word of mouth *can* be managed.
- Word of mouth *must* be managed well for a business to elevate itself to the category of legendary businesses.
- The *talk factor* pyramid, a non-academic, common-sense model, demonstrates how the "customer" or "target audience" really ought to be examined more discriminately. Actually, five levels of "target audiences" exist, each with different loyalties, expectations, and characteristics.

Section II. The Organization's Image or Reputation over Time

Figure 2 illustrates the situation addressed in Section II when you manage your business with a systematic word-of-mouth marketing effort included in the overall marketing plan. Now the company formalizes the building of its reputation using word of mouth. Now you use techniques to minimize the damaging effects of the *talk factor*, and capitalize on the powerful opportunities inherent in talk.

Figure 2

The findings introduced in Section II can be summarized as simply as one, two, three:

1. A business must take steps to stop the negative talk it generates—this will begin the reversal of a negative image or reputation.

2. A business must launch a program to generate positive talk.

3. A business must put a team in place that will keep the positive talk going so it nurtures the positive reputation.

Section III. The Word-of-Mouth Marketing Blitz

Figure 3 introduces Section III and the "blitz" to your word-of-mouth marketing plan. Let's say you've come to understand the dynamics discussed in Section I. Next you flesh out your overall marketing plan, by putting in a word-of-mouth marketing segment.

Section III tells you how to develop a "quick strike" word-of-mouth marketing campaign when launching a new product, service, or even a new idea or image.

Overall Marketing Plan for a company using a . . .

WORD-OF-MOUTH MARKETING BLITZ

The Word-of-Mouth Marketing Campaign (Blitz)

Day-to-Day Word-of-Mouth Marketing (Reputation Building)

Figure 3

The word-of-mouth marketing blitz uses the firm foundation established in your day-to-day program as a launching pad. You use the word-of-mouth marketing pyramid to focus your use of networks. And you are introduced to several new concepts:

■ The word-of-mouth marketing blitz team
■ Management using SMART objectives
■ Using "controlled outrageousness"
■ "100 little things" that get people talking

What This Book Can't *Do for You*

I've identified three things that word-of-mouth marketing *can't* do for you.

■ *Word-of-mouth marketing can't replace a marketing plan.*

If you don't already have a marketing plan, word-of-mouth marketing isn't it. You should have already deduced that from the illustrations you've already encountered. Notice that a small circle represents the word-of-mouth section in an overall marketing plan. It's a supplement. Use the techniques you learn in this book to multiply your competitive advantage, to energize your sales force, and to magnify your day-to-day effectiveness. But you must start with a comprehensive marketing plan.

■   *Word-of-mouth marketing by itself cannot work magic.*

Sorry, no miracles can come from simply reading this book—or any book. Sure, you've heard of rare and dramatic occurrences that pass for magic. I'd like nothing better than to have the president of the United States mention in a national interview that the book he last read and highly recommended was this one. Talk about powerful talk!

But remember, for every colossal success story, there's a disaster or two. For example, would you have wanted to be an importer of grapes when two or three of them were found tainted in a shipment from Chile? How could you counter the ruinous talk that swept the country within days? Word of mouth in this case was so strong, that a mother in California called the police to ask them to pursue her son's school bus and confiscate grapes from the child's lunch box! Powerful talk, indeed.

Like every other business success you've had, the successes you will achieve from using word-of-mouth marketing principles can come only after putting those principles to work. The emphasis is on *work*.

You will find as you read that, through some intuition of your own, you have always known much of what I am telling you. The best I can hope to do is to shine a light into some of the dark areas in your knowledge and to give you some workable suggestions to make order of the chaos you find in your own business. If anything, you may even have to work harder *and* smarter to achieve results using the findings you'll read about here. That's because the light I focus will reveal even more work to do if you ever want to achieve the status of a legendary organization.

But this book can be a start for you. It can be used as one more tool in conjunction with all the other resources at your disposal—your staff, your consultants, your hired professionals, your audio and video training materials, your seminars and trade magazines—all the things that make your business work.

■ *Word-of-mouth marketing can't make the dogs eat the dog food.*

Before you pull together all the lessons of word-of-mouth marketing, you must understand the first rule in marketing. Where do you go to learn this rule?

You could listen to the words of Victor Kiam, who liked an electric razor so much that he bought the company. Or you could watch my dog, Sly, eat his "Cosmic Crunch" dry food. "Cosmic Crunch" is a phony name I'll use for a nationally advertised product with different colored particles. The manufacturer said each color provided a necessary part of the dog's diet. The pitch sounded good, and the price was right, so I bought a bag of "Crunch."

Right away, I found I had invested in a dog food that had to be eaten outdoors. Each time Sly hunkered down over a bowl of his nutritious crunch, he made a mess, scattering morsels all over the kitchen floor. The dog lost weight, and I lost my patience and began feeding the animal on the back porch. Then I paid attention to what the dog was telling me. I watched him pick all the red bits of dry food from his bowl and drop them to the side.

Sly had entirely missed the point of a national advertising campaign. He was not amused by the cute animals chowing down in award-winning television commercials. He didn't even appreciate the manufacturer's idea of color coding his food so he could eat a balanced diet. How could he be so inconsiderate? I'll tell you how—Sly simply didn't like the dog food. So I stopped buying "Cosmic Crunch." The "Cosmic Crunch" company doesn't even know I stopped buying yet, let alone why I stopped. If a lot of dogs are like Sly, they might not know until the product decays on market shelves all over the country.

I recently heard Victor Kiam state the first rule of marketing much more directly in a radio interview. *"You have to have a good product,"* he said. You can't get much more succinct than that.

No matter how much you spend on advertising, no matter how clever your slogans, no matter how aggressive your sales force—you can't make it in business without a good product or service. That's the first rule in marketing.

Even this early in the book it should be obvious to you that it would be a downright blunder to launch a word-of-mouth marketing campaign for an inferior product or service. By definition, such a campaign would spread bad news even farther. So let's end this chapter by formulating a rule.

Rule One: You must have a good product or service to use word-of-mouth marketing strategies—otherwise, you'll just be spreading bad news.

Bad news, good news, no news—just what are people saying about you? Let's find out in the next chapters.

This book is organized into three sections. Section I, on the dynamics of talk, demonstrates how talk is at work all the time. Sometimes it works for you and sometimes against you, but the qualities of talk lend themselves to being managed just as any other marketing tool can.

Section II describes how the dynamics of talk can be used to improve an organization's image or reputation. This process involves three distinct operations: A business must stop negative talk; it must generate positive talk; and it must put a long-term program into place to nurture the positive reputation.

Section III tells how to use the word-of-mouth marketing blitz. This is a quick-hitting campaign created to launch a new product, service, idea, or image.

SUMMARY OF CHAPTER 1

◆ What word of mouth is and how it works is illustrated through a fictional example. Seemingly casual conversations among friends can make or break a company's reputation.

◆ Anybody can develop and use a systematic word-of-mouth marketing plan. The principles apply to all professions, businesses, non-profit organizations, and government operations. The "non-giant" company can use word-of-mouth marketing as well as any Fortune 500 corporation.

• A word-of-mouth marketing quiz is provided to awaken businesses to the negative image that word of mouth can create—usually without the businessperson even being aware of it.

◆ Rule One: You must have a good product or service to use word-of-mouth marketing strategies—otherwise, you'll just be spreading bad news.

- CAUTION: This book cannot replace a sound marketing plan; it cannot take the place of work; and it cannot sell an inferior product or service.

2

What Are Your Customers Saying about You?

Have you ever stood in a checkout line with 12 other people and wondered, "Are they ever going to open another register?"

I was standing in just such a line in a hardware store once when an assistant manager came by. I asked him if management planned to open another line. He said, "I don't know—I'm going to lunch," and left.

I stayed in line and struck up a conversation with the guy next to me. What did we talk about? Crowbars and screwdrivers? No. We chatted about what a bunch of idiots these people were. We agreed that businesses are not murdered . . . that they commit suicide by their attitudes and behavior toward customers.

In my own examinations of failed businesses, I've discovered over and over that this corporate demise is not a violent, bloody palace revolution but a slow, drawn out, self-inflicted killing.

Such companies may not even know they're dying. First they notice that new customers have stopped coming in. Then it occurs to them that old-time clients have begun staying away in droves. They make the connection that profits have been dwindling in direct proportion to customers lost. Finally, one morning they wake up and find the corpse of their dearly departed businesses.

And what is the weapon of choice for such a corporate hara kiri? Most often, it's negative word of mouth generated or aggravated by the company itself. My wife, Sherrie, and I were eating at one of those shiny, elaborate gourmet hamburger places one day. The loudspeaker system was definitely a *loud* speaker. It blared out a customer's order claim number every minute or so, and every time it did, Sherrie and I jumped. The loudspeaker (a form of talk) was so loud I almost bit off the tips of my fingers one time. Everybody in the restaurant was talking about it (a second form of talk). The manager came by to ask, "How's your dinner?" Sherrie unloaded on him. "The noise from the speakers is horribly disruptive," she said. His answer: "Yeah, everybody says that," and he walked away. A few weeks later—honestly, this is a true story—bulldozers were pushing the building into a heap of bricks. A bookstore now stands on the lot. It may not have been the loudspeaker talk that did that restaurant in, but that and the talk generated by the manager and the customers certainly contributed to its demise.

Talk as a Factor in Your Organization's Success or Failure

Like it or not, people are talking about your business all the time. Some talk is positive, but because of a quirk in human nature, negative talk reaches a much wider audience than positive talk. You cannot afford to ignore either kind—on one hand, you must take action to minimize or reverse the effects of the negative talk, and on the other hand, the potential to exploit positive talk is enormous. You *must* learn to manage what I call the *talk factor*.

The *talk factor* is simply a term to describe the fact that people talk about you, your goods, and your services. You cannot stop this talk, and you shouldn't even waste time trying. Instead, you should begin practicing the pro-active strategies to manage *what* people are saying about you. You can manage the tales people tell. You can administer damage control programs when talk creates a crisis. And you *can* initiate an active, positive program to generate favorable talk.

Listening to the "Talk Factor" Dynamics

This is as good a place as any for you to start. Open your ears. Listen. Pay attention to what people are saying. All kinds of people are talking . . . just who are they and what are they saying? Your bosses? Your secretaries? Your friends and neighbors?

Sometimes, it requires no effort at all to hear what people are saying. Remember all the talk about Chrysler Corporation going down the tubes? The closer the company got to disaster, the more the talk seemed to coalesce against Chrysler.

Customers talked about the likelihood of being stuck with cars that would not be covered by service and warranty guarantees. Suppliers talked about losing a big buyer and the inability to collect accounts receivable. Banks talked about the red ink flowing from defaulted loans. Employees worried aloud about losing jobs, pensions, and homes. Landlords talked about being saddled with empty dwellings, evictions, and repossessions. Dealers talked about losing their franchises, and livelihoods. City governments talked about the tragedies of unemployment, welfare, and other social service burdens.

When Lee Iacocca sought federal funds to save Chrysler from bankruptcy, his appearance before Congress generated talk both loud and continuous. In his book, *Iacocca*, he writes about a particular brand of the *talk factor*. Here is a quotation directly from his book:

During the congressional hearings, we were held up before the entire world as living examples of everything that was wrong with American industry. We were humiliated on the editorial pages for not having the decency to give up and die gracefully. We were the objects of scorn by the nation's cartoonists, who couldn't wait to paint us into the grave. Our wives and kids were the butt of jokes in shopping malls and schools. It was a far higher price to pay than just closing the doors and walking away. It was personal. It was pointed. And it was painful.

That's the *talk factor*. Fortunately, most of us never have to endure it at its worst—the lynch mob variety.

But the boardroom category of talk can be every bit as damaging. I was talking with the chairman of a publishing company about the powerful effect of word-of-mouth marketing horror stories.

"I know just what you're talking about," he said. "I spent a fortune on a (top-of-the-line luxury car), and it's a piece of junk. Every day something else goes wrong with it."

I never asked this executive to tell me a horror story—he volunteered it. That's a quality of the *talk factor*, too. You can bet that every time one of his colleagues gets into that car and makes small talk about "what a nice car this is," the story will be retold.

And do you suppose this publisher's company cars will ever be bought from the same dealer that supplied his personal car? I doubt it. What about his colleagues who have heard the story? Will they buy that brand of luxury car or one of the same manufacturer's cheaper models for their fleets? Again, I doubt it.

Most managers seem oblivious to what their company really looks like to others and many are most emphatically deaf to the *talk factor*. They don't even *try* to ask themselves, "What are people saying about us?" They worry about managing things—numbers and people—but don't understand that managing word of mouth might be the most important management activity of all. Why would they ignore word of mouth, a factor Regis McKenna calls "the most powerful form of communication in the business world"?

I don't think people really *ignore* word of mouth. More likely, they believe the conventional wisdom, which holds that word of mouth is beyond their control. They feel helpless to influence it. In my opinion, the conventional wisdom is wrong—*dead* wrong! The *talk factor* is managed all the time.

For example, when Apple launches a new computer product, the company manages to talk about it up front. They make sure their networks understand this new product. They talk to the user clubs, the dealers, and all the magazines. They manage the talk in newspapers, conferences, advertising, marketing, and mailings. They launch the new product with parties and brass bands. If it's a great product, within days every Apple enthusiast in the United States knows they've got another winner and they talk about the product. This talk comes down line, growing more persuasive until you find you cannot possibly survive unless you buy the new Apple product for your office. I'm one of Apple's champions. I've bought their products, and I used them in the production of this book. I encourage all my associates to investigate their systems in business.

That's the *talk factor. But that's hardly revolutionary*, you say. *Company marketers, ad agencies, and PR firms have been creating fanfare for the launching of new products forever.* Wait—there's more to the *talk factor* than that.

Next, you'll be sitting at your dinner table. You mention your new Apple to the family. Your daughter asks, "Apple? Like the kind you eat?" You explain it. Next day, she's playing with the kid next door and saying, "My dad just got a new Apple, and it may be the number one desktop publishing computer in the world—and my dad's gonna let me use it."

That's the *talk factor*, too. It's a phenomenon I call the "echo effect." Apple targets businesses with its marketing campaign, but word of mouth reverberates back and forth, spilling over to other potential users, namely children. You may not be able to control the echo effect, but you can be aware of its influence—and you can enjoy its bonus rewards.

Here's a positive example of an automobile story. Every Sunday in my newspaper, there is a review of a new car (obviously, printed talk). Then people start to talk. It works like this: I'm sitting in a restaurant and I say "John, I picked up a new Lincoln Continental and I got a *great* car."

John isn't in the market to buy a new car. But later he's talking to a buddy who's about to invest in new wheels, so he says, "A friend of mine just bought a Lincoln Continental and he's awfully happy. It was in the paper and everything. I think you ought to go look at one."

That's how the *talk factor* works. It *really* works when somebody is influenced enough to go out and buy that Continental.

Talk Can Be Scary

Everybody has a horror story about goods and services. People *love* to tell horror stories. I guess inquiring minds want to know the worst.

In fiction, writers love to talk about ghosts and werewolves and demons and evil spirits. Those things sell because people love to share horror stories. Face it, bad news sells newspapers. How often is the lead story on the front page of your paper a positive one? Not nearly as often as it's negative. What keeps the screaming exposé tabloids selling at the supermarket checkouts? Certainly it's not articles on the good done by Mother Theresa. Nope, it's the infidelity of celebrities, illegitimate births, human deformities, tragedy, and perversity. What's hot on television? Crime re-enactments and bizarre confessions. A fascination with horror seems to be part of the human condition.

In business, this predisposition takes a seemingly harmless form. People love to tell about their horrible experiences with rude clerks, apathetic waiters, and shoddy merchandise. If you're in a business involving customers—and who isn't?—you don't want to be the object of such stories. Why not? Because of the rule of 3-33.

> **Rule Two: The rule of 3-33. For every three people willing to tell a positive story about an experience with your company, there are 33 others who will tell a horror story.**

That's right, a satisfied customer might tell three people a happy story about you and your business. And yes, an irate customer might tell up to 33 others the horror story. Depending on the business, the ratio of bad to good stories varies. The White House Office of Consumer Affairs finds that a dissatisfied customer reveals the unpleasant experience to nine others. A California market research firm shows that dissatisfied automobile customers tell their stories to 22 others. A Dallas researcher says that in banking, a dissatisfied depositor will tell 11 others about a bank mistake and that those 11 will tell five more people—an average of 55 horror stories.

I use the rule of 3-33 because it's more descriptive. It isn't enough to make the arithmetic reduction and say somebody tells 11 horror stories for every good story. I find that people don't usually find more than three occasions where they can say something positive. For some reason, it's far easier to complain to somebody.

The problem is not that dissatisfied customers complain, but that they don't take their complaint to the owner or manager of the business that made them feel disgruntled. They complain to their families, friends, and co-workers. You can't afford that sort of bad advertising. The horror stories that might be told over cocktails and at lunch may easily number into the hundreds. That's the *talk factor* at its scariest.

Most of my personal horror stories concern airlines and hotels. I once called to make a hotel reservation in Las Vegas. When we came to the part about paying, the nice woman said, "Yes, we accept credit cards, but if I put this on your Visa we'll bill you $5.75 for handling the transaction." I said, "You're going to bill me for buying from you? I don't want to pay you a service charge for the right to pay you." She said, "What we would rather have you do is to send us a money order by Federal Express for the entire amount and save the charge." I said "I'm not going to be able to get a postal order at 1:00 in the morning, am I?" She said, "Probably not, sir." Then I asked, "At this point in the conversation with you, what do most people do?"

She answered, "They hang up."

Me too.

The *talk factor*.

Of course, there are plenty of positive tales too. I love the story that circulated about Nordstrom, the Seattle-based retailer legendary for customer service. This story made the *Wall Street Journal*. According to this story, an irate woman brought in a set of tires. She was adamant that she wasn't happy with those tir and she demanded her money back. So Nordstrom returned her full purchase price.

Big deal, you say? Think about this: Nordstrom does not even *sell* tires. The store took a loss on unsatisfactory merchandise that had been sold to the woman by somebody else—no arguments, no hassle. The woman simply *thought* that she had bought them at Nordstrom, so in her mind, she *had* bought them there, and the store's reaction to her demand for satisfaction would forever be the yardstick by which she measured the store—the story that she told most often would be this one, either negative or positive. The company was more concerned about managing negative talk, and more concerned about keeping a customer happy than about refusing to take back those tires. The result? A whole lot of positive talk. If you didn't read about it in the *Wall Street Journal*, you're reading about it here, right?

Now, ask yourself these questions: What would have happened to that woman in *your* store or business? Would that woman have left your premises happy? Or would she have left feeling humiliated? Are your employees inclined to argue when customers err? What kind of *talk factor* would you have generated? All too often, the talk generated would be negative.

Nordstrom and others are so concerned with the word of mouth generated by their service, you could actually say they are obsessed by it. Nordstrom will do anything to satisfy the customer, whereas most businesses will do *almost* anything.

Do you have to be a giant retailer to make such a commitment? Emphatically not. I know the world's best painter. His name is Curley, and he owns a small automobile body shop. He once painted a car, and the owner brought it back nitpicking about things that are out of a spray-painter's control—things like a run out of sight under the rocker panel. Curley listened to the litany of complaints and said, "Hold on a second." He went back into his office and returned with an $800 check, which he handed to the customer. He looked the guy in the eye and said, "Nobody could paint your car any better, but even I can't do a perfect job. Nobody can! Here's your money back because I can't afford to have you running around town telling people what a lousy job I did." I know this story is true because I witnessed it. I know Curley was absolutely obsessed with service and with controlling what people said about him. I also know that Curley is not stupid, so he would never accept another job from that customer. Finally, although the nitpicker is probably inclined to tell horror stories about businesses, he would have no basis for ever saying anything negative about Curley.

Do you think Curley lost on that $800 deal? Perhaps. But we'll never know how many more customers might never have gone to him if the nitpicker had run around town spreading negative word of mouth. If he does say anything, people probably will consider him a jerk and Curley a hero. Curley is someone who doesn't take chances. Today his shop is 15 times the size it was then, and he has a waiting list of customers. Enough said.

Remember, Most Talk Is Negative

First let me say that in general, I'm not cynical about my fellow human beings. I believe most people want to think the best about others. But inside everyone is a negative impulse that is triggered at certain times. I found one of those impulse triggers in my research for this book.

I mailed out hundreds of survey sheets asking for person-to-business experiences we could share as examples of word-of-mouth marketing. The survey sheet asked people to write about good examples as well as bad. In response, we received only a handful of positive stories. But we got back stacks of horror tales. By a ratio of 100 to 1, people seem to be conditioned to the negative aspects of the business environment—nearly everyone is willing to talk about disasters they have experienced. What does this mean to you? For one thing, it means if you really seek complaints, you can get them. For another, you have to push a lot harder at solving the negatives than managing the positives. It takes a hundred positive forces to overcome one negative.

You may not like those numbers, but they are part of the reality that is the *talk factor*. Only when you have faced up to the potential destructiveness of the *talk factor* can you begin to manage it.

Above all, remember that customers talk to and influence other potential customers. Sociologists say the average person interacts repeatedly with approximately 250 other people, including neighbors, family, and co-workers. I term this their "sphere of influence." In turn, every person in that sphere has another sphere of his or her own. There will be the obvious overlaps among spheres, but every circle will also include new members that enlarge the overall picture.

A sphere of influence is the network of people you talk to. Figure 4 shows how it would look diagrammed.

What kind of advertising do you want your customers or clients doing for your business when they interact within their spheres of influence? Do you want 99 percent of them telling the world you're a "jerk" or a "rip-off artist"? Or do you want them spreading the good word about your business going that extra mile to make them happy? Don't forget that each one of those original 250 also has his or her own sphere of influence and will probably share the information over and over again.

For now, keep in mind the idea that positive talk begins when you

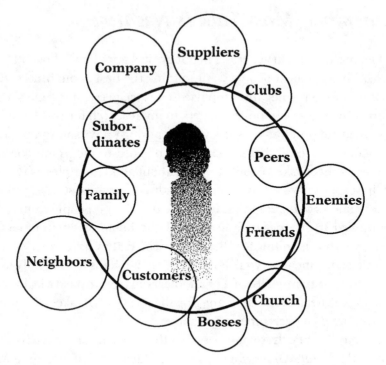

Figure 4

consistently exceed customer expectations! Remember the words of John D. Rockefeller: "Take something common and make it uncommon." Take your product or service and make it extraordinary, even legendary, and you will have mastered the first strategy for managing the *talk factor* in your word-of-mouth marketing program.

SUMMARY OF CHAPTER 2

◆   Start managing the *talk factor* in word-of-mouth marketing today by developing the acute awareness that people talk.

◆   To be a success, you'd better listen!

◆   Realize that you can't stop people from talking. But you *can* influence what they're saying about you.

◆ Recognize the cold, hard fact that people talk more about negative than positive experiences.

◆ Rule Two: The rule of 3-33—For every three people willing to tell a positive story about an experience with your company, there are 33 others who will tell a horror story.

◆ Take the initiative—start generating positive talk. The example of Apple's new computer product shows how one company does this. Later chapters address in detail the strategies to generate positive talk.

> "Do not wait for the last judgment; it takes place every day."
>
> —Albert Camus

3

The Power of Insider Talk

What's the first commandment in developing an effective word-of-mouth marketing strategy? Listen to yourself. This is so fundamental that I've written it down as another rule.

Rule Three: Listen to your insider talk!

That's right, the talk that's generated inside your own business affects the company morale, sales performance, motivation, and profit. This insider talk influences employees and outsiders, too. Believe me, word-of-mouth marketing begins inside the organization, whether you know it or not. Careless insider talk about your company is like unguided missiles flying around your offices.

To show what I mean, let me tell you about my last family vacation. It was shortly before we were to leave, and our airline tickets hadn't arrived. It was late, and the airline counters were closed so I couldn't go in and pick up tickets on this airline. But their ads say you *can* call their toll-free 800 number. And it's perfectly true . . . you can call and call and call. I tried for 45 minutes and received only a busy signal.

After midnight, it finally rang—84 times. A woman answered. I asked why my vacation tickets had not been mailed to my home. She said, "I show here on my log that those tickets should have been mailed last week, sir." I said, "Fine, we agree that they *should* have been mailed. But they haven't arrived, and we're set to travel in just a few days." She said, "Your tickets are probably stacked up with about a thousand others down in the mail room waiting to go out. They're really short-handed down there and way behind on fulfillment."

Next day, I called and talked to somebody else. I told the man I needed those tickets right away. He said, "I will personally find those tickets and express them to you by overnight mail. You'll have them tomorrow."

The next day arrived, but not the tickets. In a panic, I called again and spoke to the same man. He said, "I can't understand why you don't have them. I sent them."

The next day, and still no tickets had arrived. This time I asked somebody else to give me the control number from the overnight mailing so I could try to trace the tickets. "But sir," said the woman, "I can't find a record of them being sent. Why don't I just get another set of tickets out to you immediately?"

Indeed.

I received the tickets finally, sent by the woman I spoke to last. Most important, I learned several important lessons about word-of-mouth marketing and that airline. Let me share some of those lessons with you.

The first employee told me the truth about the airline's problems and inadequacies. The second employee lied to me, building up a great deal of ill will. The third employee revealed the lies of the second and then went on to solve my problem. I had heard through other frequent travelers—outsiders—that this airline had problems in every area, from schedules to maintenance to lost luggage. These insiders confirmed every bit of that talk and suggested even new and different inadequacies. The frustration I experienced was caused by only two people, to be sure. You might think it unfair of me to judge an entire multi-national corporation on the basis of those two contacts. And you might even say that, after all, the third employee fixed my problem. So what's the complaint? you ask.

Well, first of all, the first telephone contact led me to believe that internal functioning at that airline had been on the blink for a long time. I had heard other travelers complain, but similar remarks coming from an insider confirmed every other horror story I'd ever heard. (And you remember the rule of 3-33, don't you? People are 11 times more likely to repeat the horror stories.)

Second are the negative impressions that were branded into my memory. To the employees, those tickets were just another transaction. To my family, it was the first vacation in five years. The telephone that was busy for hours made me fume, as did the 84 telephone rings. Naturally, had I not been doing research for this book, I'd never have stayed on the line that long.

Third, I got no more than the company promised, but it took a heck of a hassle to get that. Let me explain. This airline boasted in its advertising about a toll-free number customers could call 24 hours a day. Don't you and I deserve to have that phone system staffed with sufficient numbers of people to live up to the expectations the company created? And if I have earned frequent flyer passes or have paid for tickets, don't I deserve to get them without worry that I might miss my vacation? Finally, if the process does develop a glitch, don't I deserve a little extra effort to get my problem corrected?

Certainly I do. So do you. The company didn't deliver on its promises, and that's bad enough to perpetuate the unintentional, negative word-of-mouth marketing campaign that this airline runs. But the company employees—through their insider talk—gave the campaign direction and credibility, all to the deficit side of the ledger. Powerful stuff.

Employee talk, bad or good, is extremely influential. In my opinion, it is most often the most powerful kind of insider talk, even more influential than that of executives and managers. Negative insider talk is the first thing you should teach your employees to avoid, no matter how bad conditions are. Once your employees start badmouthing you, your customers will pick it up and pass it along with even more authority, because the word comes straight from the horse's mouth.

Employees can seriously damage a company, even innocently, by letting business problems or secrets slip. When that happens, you have unintentionally launched a negative word-of-mouth marketing campaign against yourself.

Let's look at this insider talk in more detail.

Formal Insider Talk

- ■ **The Party Line.** This is the most formal, public talk generated by a company about itself. There are two kinds of party line talk:
  - • **Management Talk.** Negative talk from management is dreadfully influential. Management disagreements must be discussed in private. When problems surface in public, employees, customers, and suppliers could easily misinterpret normal managerial discussions and necessary friendly disagreements as major operations problems.
  - • **Boss Talk.** When the CEO talks, everybody listens. People are always trying to decipher what the boss really means, and reading between the lines. The boss has to set the tone for talk in the company, projecting values, honesty, and confidence. He or she must talk continually, keeping everybody informed. Being a silent, inscrutable pillar at the top of the company organizational chart is a lost opportunity for talk. The boss must keep employees informed of two situations: where the company is, and where it is going.

And what tools do members of "the establishment" use to communicate their brand of insider talk?

- ■ **Memo talk.** These are formal directives for information-sharing with employees.
- ■ **Newsletter talk.** These periodic news bulletins distribute social and business information to employees.
- ■ **Public Relations talk.** News releases and official spokesperson talk are usually intended for those outside the company, but are shared within the business as well.
- ■ **Marketing talk.** Under this heading are included sales talk and advertising talk:

- **Sales talk.** The pricing and pitching schedule intended for those on the *talk factor* pyramid. It includes all sales materials, such as brochures and sales letters. The sales representatives must know the company's products and policies. They must know their limits on granting concessions to customers. Above all, they must tell the truth—nothing generates more negative talk than lies and exaggerated promises in sales talk.
- **Advertising talk.** These are the things advertisements say about your company, its product, and its services. Make sure what you talk about in advertising is the same as what your employees see and believe. If you falsely advertise the lowest prices in town, your people will know you're a fake. They might well talk about how you rip off your customers.

■ **Training talk.** This is the formal program for teaching employees new skills, new cultures, and new procedures within a company. Make sure what you talk about in training matches the reality of what is being done every day in areas of effective sales and great service. What people are trained to do is what they do!

■ **Meeting talk.** Meetings provide oral distribution of company policy through the chain of command. Holding meetings is often essential, especially when a manager must talk to many subordinates at once. Meetings are perfect forums for introducing and sharing views on new ideas, such as your *talk factor* strategies.

■ **Financial talk.** Money talks! How a company's board or executives decide where the resources will be used is extremely influential talk. If rumors are eroding faith in your financial state, you must share enough financial information with your people to restore confidence.

■ **Signage talk.** The quality of signs and logos and the images transmitted by those symbols are crucial forms of official talk.

■ **Letter talk.** Your letterhead, logo, and business correspondence talk about you. Are you listening to your own letterhead?

■ **Switchboard talk.** The way your people answer the telephones, the quality of your hardware—these talk about your business. Customers who can't see you will talk about how they're treated on the phone. You can't depend on luck and blind faith to determine what your employees may say over the phone. You must teach them the kind of telephone talk you wish them to use.

- **Answering service talk.** This one deserves a brief mention of its own, because many otherwise wonderful small businesses aren't aware of the lack of concern, rudeness, and other negative talk generated by their answering services. If your answering service is causing you to be badmouthed, it's just as serious as if the talk had been provoked by your own employees.

- **Interviewer talk.** An interviewer screens candidates for hire after an application is completed. When he or she greets a potential employee, what he or she says, how he or she says it, and how he or she looks begin generating talk with the applicant. The company is on trial as much as the applicant.

Let's discuss some of the implications of these elements. Formal talk sets up the first line of expectations about a business. The employees learn what is expected of them from hearing through channels. Competitors see how a company is positioned. Customers interpret the talk in order to discover what they might depend on in the way of price, products, and services. Everybody who hears this form of talk translates it into the standards by which the company will conduct business. Expectations lead directly to people's perceptions.

Once expectations are established, the company's reputation is on the line. Called the "moment of truth" by many management experts, the next requirement for the business is to deliver at the point of the transaction. Here the customer decides whether the perception of what is delivered matches the expectations raised by party line talk. When the delivery falls short of expectations a gap is created. The greater the gap between perceptions and expectations, the louder will be the talk, and the greater the likelihood that it will be negative talk.

The image created by formal party line talk affects the recruitment of people to work for a business. Once an employee is hired, how well the image in formal talk matches reality, as perceived by those on the inside, will determine both the ability of managers to manage and the morale of all employees. People expect their company's interior reality to live up to the exterior presented to the public. If a wide chasm separates the two, beware of the possibilities for damaging talk.

Talk begins in the workplace. Nearly every business begins on square one with the ability, indeed the *right* to talk, to say what it stands for, what it will deliver, and how. Consumers generally will believe that what is said by a business is true. For instance, once a member of the public learns about the company—through hearing some form of talk—he becomes a prospect, someone who might try the product or service. But the instant somebody becomes a customer, the right to talk about a company becomes a shared right. Now that customer has earned the right to talk about the product, to judge how well the party line resembles reality, and how well expectations were met based on the customer's perceptions of reality.

Within a company, formal talk also shapes an employee's first impressions. That first impression, however, is re-formed every day by a number of other kinds of talk that fit under the general label . . .

Informal Talk

So much for the party line. Very often, employees, competitors, and consumers alike listen politely to the party line talk—the "words from on high"—nod as if in agreement, then walk away shaking their heads. That's because the most influential talk about a company is often informal talk.

New York business writer Robert Brody compares the formal and informal networks inside a company in this way:

Every company operates a highly visible network, thick with official, authorized information. This elaborate circuitry consists of everything from annual reports and budgets to capability statements, internal publications, boilerplate sales letters, meeting minutes, and, of course, the unsung memo. At the same time, every company also has an invisible network, all its wires humming with unofficial, mostly spoken information. It's powered by hearsay, rumors, innuendo, leaks and trial balloons—in short, by gossip.

You can evaluate a business quite well by the informal talk about it and inside it. If it matches the party line most of the time, you can feel that management is in touch with reality. If the party line can be considered the first impression, informal talk constitutes the second impression, the third, fourth, and so on.

- ■ **Grapevine talk.** The grapevine is the informal system of communication within and about a company. It's the continuous routine of talk that spreads, defines, and refines information passing through the system within the organization and in certain circles outside. Many insiders live by the grapevine, and some companies die by it.

- ■ **Rumor talk.** Rumor usually refers to a particular issue that flashes across the grapevine. This kind of talk tends to be emotional and often negative, though not necessarily. Rumor doesn't need to be substantiated by fact. It's an interesting facet of human nature that we usually demand proof upon hearing the party line from the executives of a business. On the other hand, we seldom require preponderance of evidence, let alone proof, before acting on rumor.

- ■ **Gossip talk.** Gossip tends to refer to private and personal matters. Very often gossip has a negative intent or nasty flavor to it.

In all these forms of talk, keep an ear to the ground. Don't fight the grapevine talkers and gossips by trying to stamp them out. It can't be done. Just listen and keep on clarifying. Counter with the truth at every opportunity.

- ■ **Leaked talk.** This occurs when juicy tidbits of the truth are intentionally released under a cloak of anonymity. This is purposeful talk. The leaker intends for the talk to be spread, but does not wish to be identified as the source of the talk.

■   **Opinion leader talk.** Opinion leaders are insiders who enjoy exalted status within the company. They may not have the highest positions within the company. For instance, a junior secretary who works in the executive suite might easily become an opinion leader because she has access to reliable information. A dock worker with years of experience in watching the leadership function and listening to the grapevine might hold court daily to render judgments on company matters. Younger, less experienced employees often respect an opinion leader's assessment of company matters more than a CEO's opinion, simply because the young employee might never talk to the boss.

That leads us directly into our most important category of insider talk, employee talk.

Employee Talk

I've already told you this can be a destructive force in your company. You have an expensive advertising campaign running on national television, telling customers how well you will serve them. You have hype and dollars invested in industry experts and critics. Your competitors are shaken and your prospects look good.

Then, in a hundred tiny ways, people on the interior of your own organization—insiders—start to put cracks in the exterior.

Imagine your reaction if you were a fly on the wall listening as one of your own sales representatives tells a customer, "My sales manager is a jerk to listen to the brass. This pointless new program is nothing more than a desperate attempt to win a couple of lousy points of the market share. But you and I aren't going to let that stop us from doing business the way we always have, right?" Do you think it doesn't happen? If you don't believe it, you should be reading fairy tales instead of a business book.

It doesn't have to be about a major new sales campaign to do damage, either. I heard this in a McDonald's restaurant from one of the employees, explaining why they always ran out of coffee in the refill pots in the morning when the demand is strongest. She said, "It's that night shift. They just don't care what kind of a mess they leave us when they take off right at the beginning of rush." *They don't care!* Ray Kroc would be shocked. Now don't get the idea I was eavesdropping here, hiding behind Ronald McDonald's stack of Happy Meals to catch a snatch of an ill-timed conversation. No, this woman said it loud enough for me and the other twenty people in the restaurant to hear.

How can employees be so foolish as to badmouth the organization that they should be cheerleading for? Their success is linked to yours, isn't it? Why do they act so irresponsibly? That's easy to answer. They don't know any better. And whose fault is that? Yes, it's yours. You are responsible for shaping and managing your own insider talk!

So . . . here are some tips for handling this most serious of problems from your employees, the most influential sources of talk. Make it clear to them that they are deciding the fate of the company and their own jobs by the talk they engage in. Once they're aware, highlight the positive things they should be emphasizing. Train them to say the right things.

Show that you're living in the real world, that you understand that sometimes they'll feel negative about the company policies and conditions. Show them the proper path to use in bringing those problems up for discussion with management.

Warn them not to badmouth, not even to each other on break. They can never know when somebody is listening, ready to pass on the talk and damage the company. Just tell them to break the habit completely. Have you ever seen an employee putting a telephone down on the counter while others in the store were gossiping? I know of more than one case where the badmouthing was aimed at the very customer listening on the open phone line. The best policy is to stop negative talk altogether.

Don't even permit them to badmouth the competition. If they can't say something nice, they should be quiet. Let your competition generate talk for themselves, instead of having your insiders do it for them. Badmouthing wars harm all parties involved. They take up energy that could just as well be expended on positive endeavors. You don't have to be blind to the negative side of business life but you should always create an environment that stresses the positive, more productive side.

Make it a deadly sin to badmouth to customers. Period. Establish a penalty severe enough to show you mean business. If they want to talk negatively, promise them absolute freedom of speech as a *former* employee. When I belonged to the fraternal order of Eagles, I was required to take a pledge to the effect that if I couldn't say anything positive about my brother Eagles, I wouldn't say anything at all. That's good policy for your employees about the job and their workmates.

- ■ **Check out adherence to your policy.** Call your own company. Read some of the outgoing mail. Ask your trusted customers and suppliers about what your own people are saying about you. One manager I know didn't want me to use his name, for obvious reasons—he sits in a bathroom stall with a newspaper now and then; he's not there to read—he's there to listen to what's happening in his company. Inspect what you expect . . . listen to yourself!

- ■ **Fire those who break your rule.** Negatively inclined insiders will be the ruination of you. Get rid of gripers and complainers and do it fast. I'm very serious. Negative talkers always try to recruit other, younger, more impressionable people to join their act. They are a blight on your company. Eliminate them.

- ■ **Inspire positive talk.** Find out what makes your employees happy about their jobs. Cultivate positive attitudes and enthusiastic talk at all levels in the company. People who love their jobs are the most effective ambassadors, and sometimes the entry-level workers have a great deal more positive effect than you'd think.

Notice, I didn't say here that you must issue commands to people to make them say nice things. That won't work. Naturally, your company has to be a good place to work before insiders will talk positively. An executive's job is to make employees believe in their company so much that they'll *want* to say good things. One executive secretary I interviewed said it all with, "There's nothing worse than being forced to convey a positive image when you know the company is in shambles."

- ■ **Reward those who talk positively.** If you want your employees to be positive, you should set the example in a hundred ways a thousand times every day. Give compliments. Praise the benefits of your products. Say a nice word about your suppliers and distributors. Then, when your employees pick up on this kind of talk, reward them for it. It doesn't have to be much of a tangible reward, either. Just point out the positive talk and say something like "Thanks for mentioning how professional our drivers have been. I'll pass it along to their supervisor." That's all there is to it. You could be more tangible, too. You might develop an award similar to "mental attitude" awards on youth athletic teams. Give a plaque or a trophy. Couple it with cash or time off.

One other critical source of insider talk is family talk. Spouses and children of your employees will also talk about you and your company. Generally, these important sources of talk will repeat more or less what they hear from the employee who brings home the office conversations and gossip. If you do a good job in the first place, employees' families will be in your corner.

Get to know your employees' families. Share talk with them through the newsletter by mailing it to home addresses. Send invitations to the annual parties and picnics to the house, rather than depending on getting the word out to all through passouts that might get lost before they get home. You can also involve families by sponsoring contests in your home mailings, inviting family participation.

Merchants Tire of Manassas, Virginia, puts a number code in its newsletter. Each month, a number of employees' families get a telephone call. Any family member who can tell the caller what the number code is gets a substantial cash prize. It's just one way the company stays in touch with families. It's a way of getting the family to talk about the business and to get the newsletter into the homes where information can be shared. Above all, make sure employees' families get all the *good* news (talk).

Action speaks louder than words. Say what you will, people will ignore talk if your actions contradict it. Your success in managing talk depends on backing up talk with action. Talk alone is never enough, no matter how well it's managed, in part because no matter how well you orchestrate talk inside a company, management will send one signal, sales departments will send a slightly different message, accounting will put its spin on the topic, and so on. The result is a mixed signal.

1. Victor Kiam, the electric shaver legend, shuts down the plant to talk to all his employees. It is one thing to tell people you want them to be well informed and believe in the company. It's another to stop a valuable production line and take time to show them.

2. When Mike Cohen, President and CEO of Ampere, a Chicago manufacturing company, staged a gala open house for customers to show off a new plant, he also planned a special time when employees were invited to bring their families. They were treated as VIPs—just like Ampere's customers. It's one thing to tell employees they are important—he showed them by treating them like Ampere's best customers.

3. Bob Darrah, owner of several retail stores kicked off a new sales incentive plan for all his store managers and employees. When the commissions were paid he had the office cut separate checks—calling attention to the extra reward for extra effort. In addition, he wrote personalized thank you notes to each person. Needless to say the money was appreciated but taking time to write the notes sent morale into orbit.

4. When Dick Grant took over as president of Stanley Publishing and relocated the company into new office facilities in the Chicago suburbs he wanted it to be a "new mentality" for the company. First, not one stick of their very old office equipment (desks and such) made the trip. Even more important he asked his people to adopt a new policy of a clean desk top each night. For sure they were watching him because in the past he had been the worst offender . . . with mountains piled on his desk. Now, each night he makes sure his desk top is spotless . . . not even a paper clip.

I emphasize the need for you to listen to the insider talk with the following quotation, again from Robert Brody: "Make no mistake: The invisible network will broadcast its messages, with or without your participation. Knowing what's going on in your company can be essential . . . gossip can give you the latest word on what could get you ahead—or leave you behind."

SUMMARY OF CHAPTER 3

- ◆ Rule Three: Listen to your insider talk!

- ◆ Negative insider talk is the first thing you should teach your employees to avoid. Such talk inspires an unintentional, but negative and influential, word-of-mouth marketing campaign.

- ◆ The varieties of insider talk include formal talk, informal talk, and employee talk.

- ◆ Train your people how to say the right things. Teach your employees never to say anything negative about your company, even among themselves, and not to badmouth the competition, either.

- ◆ Inspire positive talk and reward those who talk positively.

The Care and Feeding of Champions

Let's re-visit your long-held ideas about "the customer."

I'm going to share a few secrets with you about the customer. The first secret is that the customer has a split personality. In fact, he's got five personalities. You could spend a whole lifetime running a business without knowing more than just one or two of these personalities.

But if you ever expect to excel at business—if you ever want to achieve the status of "legendary" based on your delivery of goods and services—if you ever intend to capitalize on the potential of word-of-mouth marketing, you need to study the customer in greater detail. You need to learn about all these personalities.

Because it's my conclusion after a great deal of study of word-of-mouth marketing that the term *customer* is inadequate to describe the people you do business with. Those personalities I mentioned are actually five different aspects of the same customer. Each level is defined differently, and each is capable of benefiting your business in different ways. Finally, in using word-of-mouth marketing, you must employ different strategies in order to become effective with customers in each category.

These five different levels are suspect, prospect, customer, client, and champion.

I've found it extremely useful to see these levels arranged on a word-of-mouth marketing pyramid to understand them better, as shown in Figure 5. What makes the pyramid so accurate as a description is the idea that in climbing the pyramid, you find a progression from the largest group at the bottom to the smallest group—champions—at the top. You also find a closer, more sophisticated relationship between your company and the customer as you climb the pyramid and deal with higher levels.

The most important idea of all in using the pyramid as a model is that the legendary businesses either instinctively or consciously use word-of-mouth marketing strategies to move everybody from one level up to a higher level. The higher up the pyramid, the more influential the members of the segment are.

This model uses the business terms customer and client. Obviously, a doctor might use the term patient. A civil servant supervisor might use voter, employee, or member of the public instead.

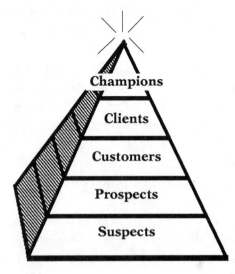

Figure 5

Let's examine each level in detail. As we go, let's concentrate on learning strategies of using word-of-mouth marketing to move the members of one segment to a higher level. Let's start learning about the care and feeding of champions.

Suspects

Definition

A suspect represents the large universe of potential prospects or customers. He or she is one of those people who have never heard of your business but who might want to know about you because he or she can use your products or services, attend your church, or donate to your fund-raising campaign.

Benefits

Statistically, the more suspects you have, the greater number you can convert to prospects, customers, and so on. You must constantly have a progression up the pyramid if the business or organization is going to grow. The company has to get the word out to more and more suspects in order to grow. Suspects cannot talk about your business because they don't know about it. You want them to talk. You want them to say positive things. You have to get the word out. The key word here is *growth*.

Threats

An obvious threat at this level is that nobody ever hears about you. But that at least can be managed with an aggressive marketing strategy. The worst threat to you among suspects is that negative word of mouth will work against you. Whether true or false, negative talk is extremely difficult to overcome.

Key Strategies

To move suspects up the pyramid, there are two key strategies:

- ■ The first is research. You must decide who your potential prospects or customers are from your lists of suspects. You must do the usual marketing research to learn the demographics (the distribution and vital statistics such as age, gender, and marital status of the individuals in the market) and psychographics (buying habits and consumer behaviors) of your target market.

- ■ Second, you need a marketing strategy that will reach out to the greatest number of suspects to tell them your story—all the great things you could do for them should they ever discover you. The name of this game is *communication* using positive word of mouth.

Most Important Activity

Let them know you're out there! It is up to you to make contact with suspects, rather than wait for them to find you.

Prospects

Definition

Unlike the suspect, the prospect knows about you from some kind of talk. Perhaps your marketing or promotion program has worked, or he or she has answered your ads, or he or she has stopped by or called because of your signs. Perhaps he or she has heard about you through word of mouth from somebody else higher on the pyramid.

Prospects have demonstrated their need for your product or service, or at least their interest or curiosity in you, by taking some kind of active step. Whereas the suspect has been passive and "unsuspecting" of you, the prospect is anybody who walks in the door, sends in a coupon, or makes a call for a quote . . . anything active to find out more about you.

Benefits

The key word here is *conversion*. Some form of word of mouth has had some effect. Now you must convert the prospect to customer. Just as no suspect can become a prospect without first hearing about you, prospects don't move up the pyramid until you get them to buy.

Threats

Again, negative word of mouth about you might be a threat, or the competition might be telling a better story than you. If either of these is true, you may lose the prospect before you've had a chance to convert him or her—that is, move him or her up to a higher level.

Key Strategies

To move prospects up the pyramid there are two key strategies:

- ■ The first impression is everything, which means the occasion of the first contact is a critical moment. If you are unable to convert a prospect to a customer, you might never get another chance.
  - When I returned a phone call to a consulting prospect, a Texas manufacturing company, the phone rang 18 times before being answered. Then the telephone receptionist patched me to the president's office where the phone rang and rang. Finally she came back on the line and said, "It appears he's not in the office—let me page him." After a lengthy wait she came back on and confessed they weren't sure where he was and did I want to leave a message? If I had been a prospect I would have doubted this company's ability to ship a product if they couldn't even answer their phones. I would have let my fingers do the walking.
  - When I decided to change my wardrobe consultant from Herb at WKRP to a professional tailor, I began calling numbers from ads in the yellow pages. Most I called gave me the facts and kissed me goodbye . . . until I called Harry Oliver. He assured me he would personally answer all my questions. Then he turned the conversation to questions

about why I was considering custom clothes, what I do for a living, and so on. In other words, the first impression he sells is probing to find the callers' interests and concerns. Then he targets his responses.

- A key strategy here is to focus everything on getting a prospect to "take a first bite" . . . Feel it, touch it, try it—drive it around block . . . no obligation and no cost.

■   The second strategy is a good sales effort. You must be very concrete in proving you can solve a prospect's problems. Show how you can meet his or her needs. Your prospects must believe they will truly benefit from the products and services you offer. Your initial step in this sales process is to qualify the prospect. To do this, use the salesperson's acronym, MAN. Does the prospect have the:

- **Means** to qualify. If a product or service is involved, does he or she have the resources to pay? If it is a volunteer project, does the prospect have the necessary time and talent?
- **Authority** to make the decision.
- **Need** for your product or service.

Most Important Activity

Without a doubt, you must dazzle a prospect with that first impression. The first contact he or she has with you must be *overwhelming*. That first experience is where word-of-mouth marketing comes to a fork in the road. The prospect has heard all kinds of good things about you. When he or she walks in, he or she either gets that overwhelmingly comforting first impression, or he or she walks away.

You don't dare let him or her walk away because he or she will be cheated out of the chance to know more about you. He or she won't get to try your product or service. Remember, the idea is to generate talk about you, talk that will bring other prospects in droves. How can that happen if you don't convert the first prospect in a convincing fashion?

Customers

Definition

The customer is somebody who has purchased your product or used your service. He or she has invested something more than a look at you; he or she has spent money or time or both.

Benefits

The key word here is *investment*. It costs a lot more to develop a new customer than it does to keep a customer who's tried your wares. Once you've made that initial investment, you must capitalize on it by making sure the customer repeats his or her business and becomes a loyal client. That means investing in something extra in order to exceed the customer's expectations.

1. When I picked up my first custom suits from Harry Oliver, he gave me a "mini workshop" on taking care of them. The explanation included using the proper hangers and travel bag. Then he proceeded to hang the suits on the proper hangers and put them in the proper travel bag . . . at no charge.

2. When I bought a selection of new fishing tackle one store concluded the sale by showing me the hottest new fishing lure in the world . . . one that was guaranteed to catch the big ones . . . and included it in my package *at no charge*.

3. Arriving late in my Monterrey, California, Doubletree Hotel room I was greeted with two warm, homemade chocolate chip cookies and cold milk along with a note as to how much they value their customers and want them to come back again. I have!

4. Mechanical Contractors built us a new steel building, doing a super job of exceeding my expectations. It was done when promised, with better than expected workmanship. The real touch was sending flowers for our grand opening.

5.   When bad weather forced a lengthy gate delay for our Delta flight they sent extra food on board and opened a free drink service. They explained they could not control the weather but they wanted to make the wait as comfortable as possible.

6.   I frequently use the Indianapolis Sheraton Northeast hotel for meetings and seminars. When they learned a group I was speaking to was having their first-ever convention they surprised all the ladies with a single rose at the Sunday morning brunch . . . naturally at no charge.

7.   We visited several churches when we moved to Fishers and most made us feel welcome. However, Pastor Joe invested the extra time to make a call on Sunday afternoon to personally thank us for attending and invite us back again. It worked!

Threats

The greatest threat is that you will begin to take the customer for granted. A customer who doesn't feel appreciated always knows he or she can go somewhere else. A customer will probably not complain to you about average or even slipshod performance. Most likely, he or she will just leave and go to your competitor. You must be consistently outstanding. Remember also the rule of 3-33—for every three people who say good things about you, there are 33 people who will talk negatively.

Key Strategies

To move customers up the pyramid there are four key strategies:

■   First, develop a relationship with your customers. People return to the same church, the same car dealer, the same grocer, the same auto parts store, or whatever, when they are able to establish a relationship. The theme music in the lead-in for the television show, *Cheers* says "You want to go where everybody knows your name," and that's what customers want. They want to go where they have a relationship with people.

■ Next, you must exceed expectations. You've must do everything they expect and much more. To exceed expectations, you first must ask questions of your customers. You must find out what their expectations are and then you must plot your strategy to consistently exceed them. When I go to Clyde, my printer, the first thing he asks is when I want it done. I normally look at my watch to give him some indication that I'm in a hurry. Clyde points to a sign on the wall that says three words: Good, Fast, Cheap. He looks at me and says, "Pick any two. If I do it well, it's not going to be fast *and* cheap. If I do it cheap, it's not going to be fast *and* good. If I do it fast, it's not going to be good *and* cheap." I may not be happy with the choices, but at least I understand them. And do you see what has happened? This printer has shaped my expectations for me, leaving nothing to chance. Clyde has managed my expectations—an important word-of-mouth marketing strategy.

■ Get your customers talking about you. You do this by "throwing gasoline on the fire" of your customers' enthusiasm. Once you have done all the nice things to exceed expectations, you do something so *astonishingly* outstanding, they can't help talking about you. And the talk they generate will be positive.

See Chapter 14 for 100 little things to get you started on ideas for throwing gasoline on the fire.

On a family vacation we stayed at the Marriott in Marina Del Ray, California, and the doorman became our guide and champion. One day we stopped to ask directions to Venice Beach and he recommended we use the hotel's free shuttle service—a freebie. They would drop us off and with a phone call, pick us up within five minutes. In addition, he suggested several attractions no visitor should miss. Then he showed Brian, my son, a couple of skateboard tricks and taught him how to do them. By the end of our stay he had indeed thrown gasoline on the fire— making everyone glad to see him on duty and at the door.

■ Finally, you must seek complaints. The more your customers complain, the more loyal they will be. Sounds contradictory, doesn't it? This is a subject so important, that an entire chapter is devoted to it later in this book.

Most Important Activity

You cannot do enough to exceed the expectations of your customers every time you deal with them. The customer, having tried your product or service, is now somebody who has a bona fide reason to talk about you. He or she is qualified to talk about you; this is where word of mouth becomes meaningful. It's one thing to have a prospect saying, "Yeah, I've heard things about them," while passing along the talk. But the customer who's tried you and says, "Not only have I heard things about them, I tried them one time, and this is the *real* story," has a credible story to tell.

Clients

Definition

A client is the continuing, loyal customer who keeps coming back because he or she believes in your ability to consistently solve problems or to meet his or her needs. Most of all, a client values the relationship with you. You can't drive away a client with a stick, unless you fail to nurture that relationship.

Clients derive as much satisfaction from the relationship as from your product or service. If a competitor moved across the street from you, a repeat customer might leave for a lower price or a new face, but a client could not walk into the other store without feeling disloyal.

Benefits

The key word here is *loyalty*. Your clients will become dependable sources of income. They will recommend you everywhere when asked. They will be emphatic allies in using word of mouth in your favor.

Threats

Just as with the customers, your biggest threat would be to take clients for granted or to become too casual toward them. You might give them short shrift in attention and service because they've been so dependable.

Key Strategies

To move clients up the pyramid there are four key strategies:

■ First, treat your clients as professional friends. Professionally, treat them as preferred customers. This segment should hear from you every time you have a special value. As friends, they should receive personal cards on their birthdays and during the holidays. Call them even when you're not selling things to them.

■ Make sure you identify them with a special field in your data bases.

■ Do something extra for your clients—every chance you get. Do things by surprise. This could be giving something free or even something personal. Once again, see Chapter 14 for some ideas. Here are some others:

- A funeral home owner regularly sends a personal letter and a carefully selected book on dealing with the loss and grief to the spouse or family.

- When we had to wait a couple of minutes for our McDonalds breakfast sandwiches the manager included complimentary hash browns . . . his way of saying thank you for choosing his McDonalds.

- When delivering a new car, one salesman always asks the proud new owner to pose with their new vehicle, using the excuse he needs the photo for a sales contest. Then he mails the photo in a display frame, along with a personal thank-you note and a box of cookies. Not only do buyers talk positively about him, they proudly show the picture he took.

- A marina and boat dealer sends a cooler, beverages, and a supply of hot dogs to new boat owners, telling them he's supplying their first picnic on the water.

- Dave Pfeiffer doesn't just repair the collision damage at his body shop. At no additional charge the car gets a complete cleanup, both inside and out as well as a complimentary wax job. His finished work often makes cars look better than new, and certainly better than the pre-accident. His repeat and referral business is at the peak of his industry.

- A travel agency surprised one of my clients at the airport as they were about to depart on a holiday trip. They greeted the family with a flight bag for each person, maps, coupons, and a supply of suntan lotion, wet napkins, and so on.
- Most of the convention group that arrived in Las Vegas for a convention had never ridden in a stretch limo. Their hotel surprised them by replacing the expected vans with limos. This was not a VIP or high roller group and they went home talking not about their winnings (or losses), but instead about this legendary hotel.

■ A key strategy would be to get your clients involved with you, to get them to help you on a project as a focus group. Ask them for their advice. Give them the chance to share their wisdom with you. That strengthens the relationship and makes it a two-way relationship. Not only do you have the superficial give and take of an exchange of goods, services, and money, but you also have shared information and trust. When these clients talk about you, they will speak of you in terms of a trusted family friend.

Most Important Activity

The most important activity with clients is to build a relationship in which you treat them as professional friends.

Champions

Definition

A champion is a person who believes in you and what you do so much he or she wants you to succeed as if you were family. Obviously, a champion is somebody who goes out and *champions* your cause. This is not entirely altruistic, however. To a champion, you are the best in the business and his or her selfish motivation is to keep you in business. He or she wants to keep you going so you'll always be able to do business with him or her.

Benefits

The key word here is *championship*. Champions don't merely talk about you, they champion your cause wherever they go. They are boosters, cheerleaders, advocates, and promoters. They brag about you and support you like family. They have developed a special relationship with you. They give you things without demanding to be repaid. And you advocate them wherever you go, too.

Threats

Your only threat of destroying your champions is benign neglect. It's the Pogo syndrome, "We have met the enemy and he is us." You must not lose contact with them. You must be sensitive to the changes in their needs. You must keep pace with them.

Key Strategies

Well, as you can see, there's no room to move any higher on the pyramid. If you want to move a champion up, marry one.

This is not as facetious as it sounds. Champions are going to multiply the benefit of everything you do. They're going to give you testimonials that are significant. They're going to give you referrals worth gold, reducing your cost of bringing in prospects, suspects, customers, and clients. In return, you must create a relationship where you meet and exceed a Champion's needs on a continuing basis.

Most Important Activity

The key with this group is to pay attention to your champions, constantly monitoring their needs and telling them you love them, and always exceeding their expectations. It goes beyond good communications—with champions, every activity must be extraordinary.

Using the Pyramid Information in Your Business

There are a number of reasons why any given segment will either stay stagnant or even slump to a lower level on the pyramid. The obvious reason is neglect—simply failing to nurture. Closely associated with neglect is ignorance—the failure to recognize that the segments exist. These are both negative viewpoints.

But let's concentrate on positive questions, the secrets of moving any segment up the pyramid. What do you have to do to convert a suspect to a prospect? To convert a customer to a client? To convert a client to a champion? Here are some simple DOs and a DON'T.

- **Invest.** Find out where your "customers" now fit on the pyramid. Spend money researching which suspects your advertising should be trying to reach. Invest in the prospects, customers, clients, and champions you already have. Spend some money on things your customers will notice and pay for.

- **Ask!** When you think about it, why not? You ask a prospect, after you've used all your other sales tactics, "What do I have to do for you to convert you to a customer?" or, "What do you want before you will become a continuing client?" or, "What kind of relationship must we have before you will become a champion for me?" When you conduct this sort of inquiry, you should try to discover the expectations of people at every level.

- **Exceed expectations at every level.** "Throw gasoline on the fire" of each segment's enthusiasm. Indoctrinate every one of your employees. If you find one of your employees not fully committed to moving your clientele up to the champion level, that employee is someone your business can do without. First and foremost, your employees must be your supporters.

■ **Treat each segment differently.** Believe me, your champions expect to be valued above everybody with less commitment than they have shown. And it's too expensive to spend the same money per suspect as you do per client. Most important of all, identify and cultivate your champions.

■ **Get everybody on the pyramid talking about you. Manage word of mouth.** The best way to do this is to dazzle at every level.

■ **DON'T get lackadaisical.** Don't take any segment for granted.

Of all these important strategies, one is so much more important than all the rest, it is stated as a rule.

Rule Four: Identify and cultivate your champions, those big hitters who will spread the word for you.

SUMMARY OF CHAPTER 4

◆ Remember that the Customer actually fits on one of five levels on the word-of-mouth marketing pyramid—suspects, prospects, customers, clients, and champions.

◆ You must research your customer base to find out where your customers belong on the pyramid.

◆ Each level has different benefits and threats to your business. There are specific strategies you can use to move customers up the pyramid.

◆ The most effective way to move people up the pyramid is to exceed expectations.

◆ The most important use of the pyramid is so that you can identify and cultivate your champions.

◆ Rule Four: Identify and cultivate your champions, those big hitters who will spread the word for you.

5

The Critical Talk Factor—Service

Let's begin this chapter with another rule.

Rule Five: Word-of-mouth marketing ultimately depends on the quality of your customer service.

If your service is legendary, word-of-mouth marketing will carry the legend to the ends of the marketplace. If your service is poor, your reputation will be, too, continually stoked by the inevitable word-of-mouth marketing that spins off the quality of your service.

Let me introduce you to a special company known for its superior customer service. It's Quill Corporation, of Lincolnshire, Illinois. Quill cultivates champions who talk about the mail order office-supply business. Quill generates its own word of mouth. And believe me, it's not mere chatter. The company is so dependable and exceptional in the delivery of its products and the service it gives, you can't help but be a repeat customer, then a client, and finally a champion.

Quill backs up its superb customer service program with action, *action, ACTION!* You already know about the industry giants such as IBM, Marriott, and Frito Lay. Those companies well deserve their reputations for superiority in their fields. The fact is, they have been studied and emulated and written about so much that it would be hard not to know of their reputations. One of the questions I always ask is this: Can the owner of a small business identify with the corporate giants? Perhaps—after all, they weren't always giants, and they do teach lessons managers at all levels can profit by.

My reason for choosing Quill as an example is the first experience I had with the company. We bought a typewriter. The typewriter arrived and wasn't used for a while because we were setting up a new office. When my national sales coordinator did begin using it, she was unhappy with it. I dismissed her complaint with "You're new, the office is new, the typewriter is new—you have to get used to it." A few days later, she stood in my office in tears. "That's a horrible typewriter, and I can't use it." I tried it and found she was absolutely correct. By that time, the warranty had expired. Still, I sent off a note of complaint to the president, Jack Miller, telling him I didn't buy a typewriter, I bought Quill Corporation. I wrote, "If you went out to try one of those typewriters in your warehouse, you would no longer sell it." My telephone rang the day that letter reached Chicago. The woman who called said, "Mr. Miller is out, but he wanted me to get back to you right away. That typewriter came in a second shipment, and it was in a batch inferior to the first one we bought. As of today, we've stopped selling any of them, and we've stopped doing business with the company that sold them to us. We'd like to correct your situation in one of two ways. Either we'll send you a better typewriter at no added cost—by overnight express, or we'll send you a refund by overnight mail. It's your choice, sir." Quill might have lost money on me that day, but I've been a champion ever since.

Quill Corporation is a family business that started in the back of a chicken store (that's right, a store where chickens were sold) with a desk, a chair, and two phones. Now this mail order house for office supplies is one of the largest in the country, employing more than 1,000 people and occupying 442,000 square feet of office, manufacturing, and warehouse space. Last time I checked, the company was opening a "Quill West" distribution office in Los Angeles.

The Quill story of actions speaking louder than words is so outstanding that I'm going to use it as a case study to begin explaining word-of-mouth marketing strategies.

As the quotation at the head of the chapter indicates, success is not luck—at least not for most of us, who realize we can't depend on winning the state lottery to achieve financial independence.

Ben Sweetland said, "Success is a journey, not a destination." Success isn't an objective or a bottom line or even a pinnacle—it's a process you live day to day. You can see it by studying the Quill Corporation's Bill of Rights. The Miller family, which runs the Illinois mail order house, has always run its business by these principles. In 1970, they set the principles down in writing to share with their customers. The interesting thing about these "constitutional" rights is that they focus not on the business, but on the customer and his feelings.

Bill of Rights

The undersigned officers and the employees of Quill Corporation express a desire to clearly state the principles and ideals which guide all of us at Quill in our relationships with our customers.

We feel this unusual step is necessary at this time because we find ourselves when we are customers— both as individuals and as a company—frequently dissatisfied with the way we are treated. Disinterest, discourteousness, bad service, late deliveries and just plain bad manners are too common.

We can't tell others how to run their businesses (except by not buying from them). But we can and will run Quill as we feel a business should be run. Therefore, the following is a list of what we consider are the inalienable rights of our customers. WE EXPECT TO BE HELD TO ACCOUNT WHENEVER WE DENY ANY OF THESE RIGHTS TO ANY CUSTOMER.

1. As a customer, you are entitled to be treated like a real,

individual, feeling Human Being . . . with friendliness, honesty and respect.

2. As a customer, you are entitled to full value for your money. When you buy a product you should feel assured that it was a good buy and that the product is exactly as it was represented to be.

3. As a customer, you are entitled to a COMPLETE guarantee of satisfaction. This is especially true when you buy the product sight unseen through the mail or over the phone.

4. As a customer, you are entitled to fast delivery. Unless otherwise indicated, the product should be shipped within 8–32 hours. In the event of a delay, you are entitled to immediate notification, along with an honest estimate of expected shipping date.

5. As a customer, you are entitled to speedy, courteous, knowledgeable answers on inquiries. You are entitled to all the help we can give in finding exactly the product or information needed.

6. As a customer, you are entitled to the privilege of being an individual and of dealing with individuals. If there is a question on your account, you are entitled to talk with or correspond with another *individual* so the question can be resolved immediately on the most mutually satisfactory basis possible.

7. *AS A CUSTOMER, YOU ARE ENTITLED TO BE TREATED EXACTLY AS WE WANT TO BE TREATED WHEN WE ARE SOMEONE ELSE'S CUSTOMER.*

Jack Miller, President

Harvey L. Miller, Secretary

Arnold Miller, Treasurer

Doing Business with Quill

When you deal with Quill, although most transactions are through the relatively impersonal means of telephone and mail, you still get the personal touch of a family business. This feeling comes through in the printed material, in the catalog, and in the contacts you have with the company employees.

At Quill, taking care of customers is company policy. It starts at the top with the president, Jack Miller.

"We're a company selling basic commodity items available from 15,000 other companies throughout the country," he says. "Yet we're the very largest in the industry. Customer service is not done well in other places, and we wanted to make a declaration that in our company, that's the way it's done."

To the Miller family, that declaration is their customer "Bill of Rights," written 1970 and published on the cover of their mail order catalog. Since then, it's been in every catalog. The "Bill of Rights" states the basic beliefs of the Millers about how a business ought to be run. And Jack Miller believes the reason the company has grown so much is a direct result of the policy.

"There are huge blow-ups of the 'Bill of Rights' in every department in the company," he says. But Miller knows that signs stating the policy alone do not make a policy work.

"It's not something you put into a report once a year. It's something you live and you breathe every day all day long."

Here are some of the highlights of the Quill company's attitudes and philosophy toward achieving business success by delivering superior customer service. The words are all Jack Miller's.

The Quill Business Philosophy

"You don't get wealthy trying to maneuver deals. You have no God-given right to prosper. You have to earn it day in and day out. You're successful in business by satisfying a customer's needs and wants. One of those is the want for being well treated, for being dealt with honestly and for being spoken to in a civil way."

Service—Bad or Good—Makes You Passionate

"When I go to a restaurant, I don't care what the food tastes like—to me, it's gasoline that keeps my body running. But I sure care about the service, the waitress, how I'm treated. I was in a restaurant in Zurich, Switzerland, one time and the waitress was so perfect, I had to ask her if she was always that nice to her customers. She said, 'Why shouldn't I be? You're my guest.' It's just a question of caring, of taking care of people."

Good Service Is Simple

"You know what it takes to make it in the plumbing business? All you'd have to do to be a success is to show up on time. There isn't a plumber in the country that shows up on time. They say they'll be there at eight-thirty, and the person stays home but the plumber doesn't show up until eleven. It's simple consideration that you show up on time. You leave the house as clean as it was. You guarantee your work. You be pleasant. That's how you make it in the plumbing business . . . in any business."

The Policy Starts at the Top

"If there is a decision to be made, people will decide based on what they've seen the boss do. So you have to set an example for the managers. With our people we say, 'Look, if you've taken care of the customer, you've made the right decision.' I don't see any other way to do it.

"If you really believe it and internalize it and make it a part of your everyday life, judge everything else by it, then there's no way it won't be done in the rest of the company."

Customer Service Affects ALL Policy Decisions

"Our customer service policy is an indoctrination to our employees—it's like a religion. If some manager comes in with an idea to save us a bunch of money, say $5,000 a month, and you have to ask, 'What will it do for our customer service? How will it improve that? Will it hurt customer service?' If it's going to hurt us in customer service, maybe we won't want to save the $5,000."

If You Make a Promise, You Keep It

"One of my managers told me that we missed an air shipment to Texas. It was promised, but he said the order would have to wait until next day. I asked why we should wait. He said if we used any other way, it would cost us $250—more than the profit we were making on this order. Who the hell cares? We promised the customer. It's our fault, not his. We shipped it. If you can't do something, that's a different story. You tell the customer you can't. But you have to keep your promises."

Customers Pay Your Policy Back in Kind(ness)

"When something goes wrong with this company, people don't stop dealing with us. They sit down and they write, 'Dear Jack, something happened with my last order, and I know you don't want to run your company this way.' . . . It gives us an opportunity to respond. Everybody that calls to complain to me, I talk to. I have somebody in customer service write back to customers who complain, but I check the response to every letter."

The Bottom Line

"Customer service doesn't cost a lot of money. If you're arguing with a customer about whether you're going to take something back, you're going to lose that argument.

"In the mail order business, it costs us $15 to $20 to acquire a new customer who makes that first order. The only way we're going to *make* money is by repeat business. I'd be absolutely out of my whack not to love these people."

I love that line. It reduces the entire point of this book to the simple, blunt explanation of why *legendary* customer service is essential to extraordinary business success, why no business can ever reach its full potential without superior service, and why word-of-mouth marketing depends on the quality of service. Let me repeat the thought in a paraphrase. Every business person should repeat this sentence like a morning prayer and before opening his or her mouth to deal with a customer: "I'd be absolutely out of my whack not to love this customer."

Before leaving the example of Quill to discuss a number of principles that will help you transcend the gap between ordinary customer service and great customer service, I'm going to list a number of tips from the company. You could take every one of these ideas and apply them to your own business. Some of them might cost a bit of money to initiate, but you should consider any cost an investment in your potential greatness.

First, put your attitude toward customer service and your promises in writing. Write a contract with your customers. Then display the contract. What you'll be doing is committing yourself and your employees to action. You'll be setting the tone for doing business. If you're the type who exudes self-confidence, you could simply borrow Quill's words and develop whatever adjustments and additions that fit your business.

You'll be saying to your customer, "This is the way we work. We feel so strongly about giving you great service that we're willing to put it into writing so you can hold us to account. Go ahead and make my day by exercising these rights."

This is the first step in opening your doors to customers who might have a complaint but who never complain. You're saying loudly and clearly, "Don't leave us without first exercising your rights."

Well, there's the Quill story. You can learn a lot of the dynamics of word-of-mouth marketing from it. In the coming chapters we'll look at a system that will take your business from the realm of awful or neutral word of mouth and turn on the positive word of mouth. When you're finished looking over these strategies, you'll understand how a legendary "non-giant" company like Quill has earned its niche in the hearts of its customers. You'll see how the underlying philosophy of delivering great customer service is the force behind the best use of word-of-mouth marketing dynamics.

What about the giant companies?

Some gargantuans pay only lip service to customer satisfaction. You read their ads and see and hear their commercials on television. Then you try their products or meet their people and wonder how they can make such claims. You shrug your shoulders and figure that all that great customer satisfaction must be happening out in the tar pits in California, the geysers of Wyoming, or the swamps of Florida. You know for sure that all that satisfaction hasn't been happening in *your* household.

Westinghouse Furniture Systems, of Grand Rapids, Michigan, offers a refreshing story. This unit of the Westinghouse Electric Corporation, which has nearly $13-billion-a-year in sales put its money where its corporate mouth is in 1984 by creating a vice president of customer assurance. John Dorman now holds that position at Westinghouse Furniture Systems, which designs, manufactures, and markets office systems, furniture, and components.

"We have a high volume of repeat business, so a positive reaction from our customers is critical to us," Dorman says. "Also, our business is specified by architects, interior designers, facility managers, and dealers. They're the ones who talk about us to the consumers of our products. If we don't make a positive impression on them, we will be losing our chance to compete. Word of mouth is critical."

More critical than advertising? "We don't have a big advertising budget. We rely far more on word of mouth. Advertising is important when we want people to understand who we are. After that, we have to convince them we're the total customer assurance leader."

Dorman offers proof that service and quality pay off. "We landed a Chrysler Corporation contract after Chrysler conducted a 19-month study of all major furniture vendors in the industry. When it was all done, the concepts of quality and customer partnership we espouse are what got us the contract. We don't carry the broadest line and we're not the largest provider. But Chrysler's study said we were the best. This was a quality assurance story that turned into a major business accomplishment."

There you have it—the purpose of word-of-mouth marketing reaffirmed—a flat statement that word of mouth is a critical factor that depends on customer service, and confirmation that the payoff comes in the form of a return on the bottom line.

The following are Westinghouse Furniture Systems' recommendations for starting or improving a customer assurance program:

■ Obtain the absolute dedication of the executive management team. As pointed out in the earlier chapter about insider talk, less than total commitment from executives will only hurt company morale.

■ Identify your customers, focusing especially on those people within a company who make or contribute to the buying decision.

■ List each customer's expectations. Define your methods of meeting those expectations. Make sure your methods are clearly stated, concrete, and understood by everyone involved.

■ Set up a performance measurement system for all employees. Use rewards for improvements in performance that are tied to customer's needs and expectations.

- A Florida appliance retailer regularly has mystery shoppers pose as customers and make purchases in his parts department. Sales people who follow his specific five steps for meeting and greeting customers are rewarded with a day off with pay.

- Ramada Inns just mailed stickers to their thousands of frequent guests who hold a Ramada Business Card, a method for guests to accumulate frequent stayer points and rewards. The stickers are to be handed out to any Ramada hotel staff person demonstrating "above and beyond" service. The stickers have a scratch and win area, offering Ramada employees instant prizes. In addition they can turn the stickers in to be in drawings to win cash—as much as $250.

- One grocery chain has a "Catch our employees doing something extra" program. Comment cards are available throughout the store and each employee wears an oversized name tag allowing customers to see their names. The cards can be dropped in one of several boxes around the store, or mailed free. For each card returned, the employee named receives a gift certificate good for $5.00 at any of several area restaurants.

■ Create a communication vehicle that regularly focuses employee and management attention on the objectives.

■ Make continued improvements in performance through problem solving and positive action. A positive trend in performance is the main goal. Absolute statistical objectives are secondary, with improvements becoming visible only after the employees accept a customer-oriented approach and recognize their role in contributing to it.

Michael Maccoby of Harvard University, author of *The Gamesman and the Leader*, has studied Westinghouse and calls the company "one of the five real customer-focused businesses in the world."

In the next section, we'll examine more closely the strategies and principles that make companies such as Quill and Westinghouse Furniture Systems legendary in their industries.

SUMMARY OF CHAPTER 5

◆ Rule Five: Word-of-mouth marketing ultimately depends on the quality of your customer service.

◆ Often people remember your service more distinctly than a product.

◆ You need a "Customer Bill of Rights." This establishes the philosophy of your company. It's not a bad idea to emulate Quill Corporation's.

◆ Good service is simple and starts at the top. You have to keep the promises you make to your customers.

◆ Besides generating positive word of mouth, great service brings people back. It's more cost-effective than programs to acquire new customers.

Word-of-Mouth Marketing over the Long Run— Building and Maintaining the Company Reputation

6

Stop the Horror Talk—Defusing Angry Customers

In the first section of the book you were introduced to the dynamics of talk and the most critical factor in word-of-mouth marketing, customer service. This section tackles the task of using those dynamics to build and maintain a company image. The section gives logical steps you can follow in turning an awful company image around.

Your starting point is to address the quality of your customer service, turning around the effect of horror talk about your company. Next, you will concentrate on establishing a pattern of positive talk. Then, you will learn a method of word-of-mouth marketing research by seeking out complaints. Armed with information from your research, you will then decide on the image you want to cultivate—in other words, you will

Negative Word of Mouth	No Word of Mouth	Positive Word of Mouth
Awful Service	Good or Adequate Service	Great Service

Figure 6

define the goal of your word-of-mouth marketing program. Finally, you will learn a system that will help you to get things done.

One important idea for you to visualize is that word of mouth operates on a continuum from negative to positive. That continuum, shown in Figure 6, is directly related to the quality of service delivered.

Another important rule should occur to you as you progress through this section, with its emphasis on customer service to set up a climate for positive word of mouth, marketing research, employee management, and management techniques.

Rule Six: Word-of-mouth marketing cuts across every organizational and operational division in a company.

That's right, you can't isolate responsibility for word-of-mouth marketing in the marketing or public relations department. Just as legendary customer service doesn't begin and end in the customer service department, responsibility for word-of-mouth marketing rests with every manager, executive, salesperson, and line worker. Every department must make it a major consideration in policies and practices. Remember how widespread all the kinds of formal and informal talk can be in your company? You cannot isolate the effects of word of mouth.

The first thing Jan Carlzon did to turn around Scandinavian Airlines was to get everybody involved with his vision. He communicated personally with groups of his employees in hangars everywhere the airline served. He communicated in other ways, too. In his book, *Moments of Truth*, he writes:

> Beyond the attention to service, we were also able to stir new energy simply by ensuring that everyone connected with SAS— from board members to reservation clerks—knew about and understood our overall vision. As soon as we received approval from the board, we distributed a little red book titled 'Let's Get in There and Fight' to every one of our 20,000 employees. The book gave the staff, in very concise terms, the same information about the company's vision and goal that the board and top management already had. We wanted everyone in the company to understand the goal; we couldn't risk our message becoming distorted as it worked its way through the company.
>
> There is no question that by diffusing responsibility and communicating our vision to all employees, we were making more demands on them. Anyone who is not given information cannot assume responsibility. But anyone who is given information cannot avoid assuming it.

Keep this sixth rule in mind as you examine how to stop the most damaging word of mouth of all, that generated by an upset customer.

As we've already discussed, people love to tell horror stories. Those kinds of negative word-of-mouth tales can ruin a business. The more striking the story, the greater damage it can do. And every story is magnified in direct proportion to the level of a customer's anger. The madder you make somebody, the greater will be the exaggeration, the spite, and the desire for revenge in telling of the story. You simply cannot afford to be awful in business.

So what is the standard by which we measure the good, the bad, and the awful? I have a simple rule by which I gauge my performance. If I have caused a customer to become angry, my performance has been awful in some way. *The first thing to do is stop everything and fix that customer.*

Don't bother looking for blame or fault. Don't worry about overhauling the business or firing half your staff. Just defuse the fury of your customer. Once that is done, you can spend all the time you want in analyzing and solving the cause of the problem.

Remember, start by defusing the furious customer.

You can do that by using five steps, a proven common sense course in human relations that requires fewer than 25 words—21, to be exact. Here are the five steps to defusing problems. I call them the . . .

Five-Breath Method of Defusing Customer Fury

BREATH 1: Acknowledge the person is upset.

BREATH 2: Make a sad/glad statement.

BREATH 3: Make a positive statement.

BREATH 4: Ask the "magic question."

BREATH 5: Make a settlement.

When you have done these things, you will have preempted a flurry of negative talk. Isn't that simple?

It *can* be as simple as that, or defusing an upset customer may be as complicated as any other matter of life and death. Sometimes you can run a business perfectly, eagerly adopting every customer service principle ever devised. You can embrace every bit of conventional wisdom like a politician kissing babies. You can be sincere about it, too, standing behind your products, services, and policies—you can be wise enough to take every bit of advice I offer. You can be as personable as Dale Carnegie or Will Rogers and still things will go wrong. Despite your best efforts, your customers may misunderstand you or perhaps even dislike you, and they will spread negative word of mouth. In addition, your employees might sometimes misunderstand your policies or simply have an off day and make your customers angry, giving rise to negative word of mouth. Or the employees will follow your practices to the letter, and customers will misunderstand on their own initiative.

Maybe an irate customer's behavior cannot be explained by anything more rational than Elbert Hubbard's observation, "Every man is a damn fool for at least five minutes every day . . . "

Every woman, too. But you must also remember that the irate customer may have good reason to be angry.

Let me give you an example from my own experience. I knew someone was annoyed the second I heard all four tires screeching as a car fishtailed to a halt in the parking lot outside my retail store. A woman left the car door open and stormed inside. Seeing her, two of my clerks remembered things they had to do in the back of the store. A third clerk demonstrated his psychic abilities by picking up the telephone and taking an order without the phone even ringing. The fourth clerk hadn't been paying attention and didn't notice the onslaught until the petite woman pointed her finger at him. Her words were just as pointed: "I want to see the boss. Where is he?"

Great, I thought. I'd just finished a training session with this crew, a session on how to defuse an upset customer. The other three had flunked their first test, but this man was my best salesperson. I eagerly awaited his response.

He smiled—a good start. Then he turned and pointed at me. She pounced.

I vowed there would be more and better training and maybe lessons in bravery for this crew. But the woman didn't give me much time for thinking, let alone talking.

The conversation was pretty well balanced. She would scream at me a while and I would say, "Yes, ma'am," or "No, ma'am." Then she would scream again.

I tried to use my never-fail Five-Breath Method. Step one, I remembered, was: Acknowledge the person is upset. I said, "I can see you are mad." This demonstration of my absolute mastery of the obvious brought a snicker from clerk number four and a little choking sound from her throat before she renewed her attack.

After a few customers had stepped into the store, heard the uproar, spun on their heels and marched right out again, I somehow managed to make the suggestion that we go into my office to continue the conversation. The last thing I needed was for this scene to lead to other customers talking. She led me to the office as if it were her own and slammed the door behind us.

She vented her anger on me for thirty minutes. For the first time I could remember, none of my employees needed to disturb me in the office.

The woman's story was not that she was unhappy with any of our products, but with our delivery service, although she wasn't even a customer. It seems that she'd been walking across the parking lot of a shopping mall, and one of my delivery trucks had been speeding by. The truck had nearly hit her three-year-old daughter. She said she was extremely angry and insisted that she had every right to be. Did I want to dispute that?

Well . . . no, ma'am.

Finally I knew the source of her fury. I agreed that she had a right to be angry, and told her I would have been just as upset (maybe even more upset) had the same thing happened to me. I skipped right to Step Four. I asked the magic question, "What can I do to make you happy?"

She demanded an apology from the driver. Believe me, she got it, on the spot and in exactly the words she wanted. After she left, the driver had a private audience with me. This had been the third complaint of his speeding. Unhappily, I fired him for not having responded to earlier warnings and before he could present our business with something worse than an upset customer—a bereaved customer.

Nobody can give you a sure-fire formula that will solve all your problems or soothe all your upset customers. But the five-step system will help minimize most of your problems with irate customers, because the system employs two ingredients almost everybody treasures, respect for others and the all too uncommon common sense.

Let us look at these five proven steps in detail. In case you're wondering why I've labelled them as "breaths," the idea is to take a deep breath before speaking. Breathe, pause, wait, and then speak. The process allows the angry customer the first words, or the choice to stop speaking if he or she wants to. You simply use the moment to listen, to nod, to avoid interrupting, and to choose the precise words you're going to use. That's all. It may seem a little thing, but it's very worthwhile, believe me.

BREATH 1: Acknowledge that the person is upset.

Stop!

Take a breath. If it is your turn to talk, fine. All you have to say is, "I can see you are upset."

This is just common sense! Being upset enough to complain is not easy for most consumers. The least you can do is pay attention and be kind. When somebody is angry, notice!

You see, it takes no effort at all for you to make a person angry. You start by giving him or her an expectation. Then you frustrate the person by failing to meet that expectation. Then you can sit back and watch the body as it goes on automatic, pumping adrenalin into the bloodstream, stimulating the body and brain until the results appear in the form of flushed color, narrowed eyes, tightened jaws, stiffened body—the emotion we call anger. Nothing to it.

Think about how much effort it requires to direct that anger into the form of a complaint. Think of the courage it takes for most people to complain. It's a simplification of the psychological process, but generally the first step a person must go through in sorting frustration is to decide whether to: a) suppress the anger and suffer it internally; b) direct the anger irrationally at somebody or something handy—maybe by smashing the troublesome toaster he bought from you; or, c) complain to you. Some market research indicates that fewer than one in ten customers will take the trouble to choose the third option and complain. This is, therefore, a rare case and somebody worth your trouble. When that customer calls, writes, or comes in, he has already made a number of choices. *And you had better pay attention!*

Here's why you had better pay attention: The customer who complains has already chosen *not* to overlook the flaw in your product or service, however minor.

A woman may not send her cross-eyed, illiterate husband back to her mother-in-law, deciding she can live with his ill manners and odd odors. But if she has come to complain to you about the dryer you sold her, it doesn't matter whether the problem is clothing cinders plastered inside the drum or simply a timer that ticks too loudly. She has already decided she won't live with it. Recognize that fact up front. Later, I'll tell you what to do about it.

The customer who complains has already chosen *not* to cool down on his or her own. He or she is committed to talking!

The act of walking or driving to a business, sitting down to write a letter—"Fire off a note of protest," as the news magazines would say— or even just dialing your business phone number will often cool a person off. If a customer has gotten past that to make any kind of contact in person, he or she does not want to be put off. He or she expects you to help him or her cool off. He or she thinks it's your job. It *is* your job, and you should recognize it.

The customer who complains has already decided not to be afraid of looking foolish. Let me tell you about the backwoods hermit who made his annual trek from the wilderness to buy one of "them newfangled chainsaws." A month later he surprised the trading post owner by returning with the battered saw to demand a refund. The trader asked, "What's wrong with it?" "It don't work right," said the hermit. "I done cut two cords of wood before I went back to my hand saw and done better with that." "Well let's have a look at what's wrong," said the trader. He yanked on the starter rope, and the saw engine fired up instantly. "What's that noise?" yelped the startled hermit.

The customer who decides to complain has overcome the fear of looking silly. Still, he or she is wary, even on edge, waiting to react to your reaction to the complaint. You owe the customer a respectful reaction—even if the fault *isn't* your product's or service's. You wouldn't fire these words back at an irate customer, "Boy, are you stupid." No, but sometimes your reaction, even body language, can be just as offensive as those words. The safe response to a customer with a complaint is to acknowledge their anger.

A customer complaint is an investment. Don't waste it!

None of the foregoing even considers the customer's loss of time, the logistics of travel, the attempted re-folding (it can't be done) or attempted repackaging of your product (it never fits back into the box), or picking through the trash for the price tags and receipts that have already been thrown away. It doesn't account for the mental rehearsal of the arguments the customer plans to use on you. Not to mention the threats of lawyers or baseball bats that have been considered or even brought along for moral courage. Finally, your irate customer might have cooled off in coming over or calling, requiring a regeneration of anger. The customer has already invested this and more into making a complaint. He or she is a Rodney or a Ms. Dangerfield looking for a little respect. Give it. Just say, "You're angry." BREATH 1: Acknowledge that the customer is upset.

Now, take another breath and go on.

BREATH 2: Make a sad/glad statement.

All you did in Breath 1 is show a little respect for the trouble the customer has taken to complain. All you did was listen. Then you said, "I see you are upset." In the next breath, express your regret and pleasure. Say, "I'm sorry you had a problem, and I'm glad you called it to my attention," or something similar. Is it any wonder if a customer pops a cerebral circuit breaker the instant he or she registers a complaint and hears any of the following few DON'Ts?

"Who did you speak to?" (Even if you say "whom," he's gonna be mad.)

"Who waited on you? Are you sure?"

"What's your account number?"

"Refunds and exchanges are not handled in this department. That's done at our annex across town."

"Can you call back later?" (Meaning, "I get off in five minutes.")

"There's nothing I can do about it—company policy." (With or without a "sorry.")

"The person who handles that is out. Can you bring your refrigerator back in the morning?"

"The computer fouled up. . . ."

"The service department. . . ."

"Our vendor. . . ."

"She. . . ."

(Or my all-time least favorite, the silence that comes from ignoring an angry customer—the invisible treatment.)

Great customer service and the positive word of mouth it generates often means more than just fixing problems. It often means fixing the customer, too. In this effort, a little caring goes a long way.

The customer expects you to care. So *care!*

BREATH 3: Make a positive statement.

The first two steps have used only two breaths, perhaps even one. You have said, "I can see you're angry. I'm sorry you had a problem, and I'm glad you called it to my attention." Now you will have time for another breath. You will have stunned your irate customer. People nowadays have grown so accustomed to hassles from bureaucrats, merchants, clerks, and sales reps, they expect to be hassled. If you do anything kind or considerate, instead, you will surprise them. If you've told an irate customer you care about the person's needs, you've already begun to turn the tide of fury. So imagine the shock you'll create when you make a positive statement with your next breath—something like: "I will get something done about your problem."

Wow! On top of "I care" and "I respect you," you have just said, "I will act."

For three days a hotel in Cincinnati was my home, and a happy change it was from many lousy nights I'd spent in other hotels and motels in cities across the country. Everything I'd read about this small chain and the owner's passion for delivering the goods to guests was true. Well, there were a couple of minor exceptions. The one that irked me temporarily was the breakfast order I'd filled out and hung on my room doorknob. The next morning, I called to ask why the hot coffee and toast I'd ordered were an hour late. Room service had forgotten the order.

Because I'm in the business of customer service, and always looking for new ways to make word-of-mouth marketing work, I always make customer comments. Usually, I think, the comment and suggestion cards leave the room in the care of maids and busboys, carried in green, extra-tough plastic bags to incinerator fires. That wasn't so at this hotel. The owner personally replied to my written comment, and not by a form letter, either. Item by item, he responded to my remarks, explaining the action the staff had taken to correct the faults. What did it cost him to make this explanation to me? A little time spent giving directions to his staff and signing a note? A stamp and stationery? What did it gain him? My respect and my business—I will stay at that hotel whenever I stay in Cincinnati.

Besides, although the hotel hardly needs the advertising from me, I still talk about my pleasant experience with them when I give seminars across the country. Word of mouth.

BREATH 4: *Ask the magic question.*

You've used three breaths. In the first two, you said, "I can see you're angry. I'm sorry you had a problem, and I'm glad you called it to my attention." The next breath you used to say, "I will get something done about your problem." The upset customer will give you time for a fourth breath as anger turns to shock. Then you can ask the magic question: "What will make you happy?"

Five words, you mutter incredulously. Magic? you may ask rhetorically. Hogwash, you may say disdainfully. Perhaps I do exaggerate a little, but only a little. If the question is not magic, it surely has magic in it. Why? Because those five words are packed with positive connotations. The first positive connotation is the emphasis on to the customer. It says *your* needs, *your* problems; not me, but you, You, YOU!

The second positive connotation is happiness. The question implies that the customer will not be a loser in the ensuing personal interchange. The question indicates an interest in changing the anger acknowledged in earlier steps into positive feelings. You may feel that asking such an open-ended question will lead to such responses as:

"A check for a million dollars would make me happy," or "Instead of exchanging this hairbrush, I want you to sign the store over to me—it's the only thing that will make me happy," or "Gimme your first-born," or the customer simply hands you a blade and asks you to show some of your own blood.

Well, I admit if you ask such an open-ended question, there is always the possibility that your customer will say those things or things just as unreasonable. But, I must disagree with the notion that people are out to cheat you when they buy from you. Customers almost never ask for something that costs nothing—not in my experience. They spend money in good faith, expecting good products and services in return. If the expectations aren't met, they have a further expectation that an honorable business representative will correct the problem through some reasonable action. The emphasis is on *reasonable*.

Most customers are reasonable. Most customers don't cheat. People who think otherwise ought not to be in business. It can't be fun to serve customers with excellent products or services if you live in constant fear and anxiety of getting cheated! The late John Bremner, professor of journalism at the University of Kansas and former consultant to the entire chain of Gannett newspapers, which includes *USA Today*, used to say this to reporters, editors, and journalism students: "Better to be fooled once in a while than to be constantly suspicious."

He was talking to people in a field often considered the most cynical in America, with its investigators, critics, analysts, pundits, and essayists. If he could give such advice to the men and women who have to deal with criminals, flacks, marketeers, lobbyists, politicians, and bureaucrats over the very issues of truth and falsehood, why can't we in business borrow from the wisdom? Let me illustrate in a story about spilled oil.

Before we'd taught our parts employees how to defuse problem situations, I visited our Henderson, Kentucky, store and found the manager in an argument with a customer.

I got the gist of the dispute in a hurry. The customer claimed the store had sold him the wrong oil filter for his car. The rubber gasket on the oil filter had not sealed properly, and the car had dumped its fresh engine oil immediately after starting. The manager threw up a defensive shield like no NFL quarterback had ever seen. He held up the contested invoice and pointed out that the customer had bought three different filters. He told the customer, "You installed the wrong filter on your car."

Wrong, indeed. Not only was he arguing with the customer, but by inference he was calling him a dope who didn't even know how to install an automobile oil filter. The words "upset" and "irate" do not adequately describe what this customer was feeling. His words cannot be repeated here. But he did express a certain dismay at being called an incompetent, and he did mention he would not return to patronize this store during his lifetime.

The manager hardly cared, and it showed. When the phone rang, I stepped up, offering to handle the situation. The manager gladly took the telephone call. I used the first three steps in my program to settle the customer down a little. I learned from him that five quarts of oil had sprayed all over his garage floor. Then I asked, "What can we do to correct this problem? What will make you happy?" The store manager nearly bit the mouthpiece off his telephone receiver when he overheard my suggestion that we would make this customer happy at any cost. I was leaving myself open to a claim that the man's engine had been destroyed by running without oil and that we were responsible. That was not what I said, mind you, but this manager was hearing things that day anyhow. After using these defusing steps, the customer eagerly responded to my question, "What will make you happy." "I want another oil filter," he said. "And this time, I want the right one. That's what I've been trying to get across to this . . . this . . . manager for the past fifteen minutes." The customer wasn't out to beat us. He just wanted the correct filter, a fair and reasonable request. Our manager was either in fear of big legal problems, or he was letting his ego get in the way of the transaction—he wouldn't admit that he could have sold the wrong filter. So I went right to . . .

BREATH 5: *Make a settlement.*

I gave the man the filter he wanted—it didn't matter whether he'd actually made a mistake in installing the first one. What was the point of arguing if I could keep a regular customer coming back? More important, in terms of word-of-mouth marketing, what was the possibility that we could prevent him from talking about us in adverse terms, from telling 33 people what idiots we were at our parts store? (You don't think he'd admit his fault to others if he did install the wrong filter, do you? That's not one of the dynamics in word-of-mouth marketing.) All he wanted was a filter.

If you're with me so far, you'll agree that the negative situation had been neutralized. The things I did probably prevented a horror story being told about us and the awful service he perceived. If you believe in the rule of 3-33 and the power of word-of-mouth marketing, we probably prevented up to 33 negative stories from being told about us.

Now is the perfect time to add a sixth step to repairing the negative word-of-mouth situation. Now you can go beyond a neutral situation and turn the customer's aggravation to your own advantage. Now is the time to do something extra.

The BONUS STEP: Do something extra and unexpected.

In the case of this customer, I gave him five quarts of oil to replace the ones he'd lost and I added some supplies to clean up his garage floor. My bet was that he'd be back to this store, and that he'd tell at least three other people about the fair treatment he'd received.

What happened here? Not much, really. I simply told the customer in words and actions, "I'm sorry. Your point is well taken. Your request is reasonable. I'm going to give you what you ask—*and a little more.* We want to keep you as a valued customer." I did it in five easy breaths, consuming no more than a few seconds. In those seconds, I restored order to a very emotional situation . . . and, I might add, one that needn't ever have reached the level of anger and shouting that it did.

Fine and dandy, you say, the guy wanted a lousy oil filter. What if he had been sold an incorrect filter and had run the oil pan dry at 55 miles an hour? What if the hot engine had seized up on the highway?

These are tough questions, and you are right to ask them. In this age of product liability suits and the enormous damages awarded by courts to plaintiffs making (in some cases) the most outrageous claims, I can see your point in asking. My favorite, true example in the ridiculous claims and awards department went against the ladder manufacturer whose product went to a farmer's barn one winter. The farmer stood the ladder on a frozen manure pile and climbed to the loft all winter to throw down hay bales to his livestock. In the spring, the dung heap warmed and would not support the ladder. It slipped; he fell. He sued and won because the manufacturer had not foreseen the need to print (on the dozen or so warning labels already tacked onto his ladders) that there was a danger in resting the ladder on melting dung heaps.

To answer your questions about the possibility of a ruined engine in the light of my question to the customer; first, I did not promise to give away the store when I asked the customer what he wanted to correct the situation and make him happy. The store manager may have heard that in my question, and you may have read it that way, but it was not what I said.

After creating a suitably civilized environment for discussion with the first three breaths, I was merely trying to establish a negotiating position for the customer. If his request was entirely reasonable, which it almost always turns out to be, I intended to meet the demand and save the customer for the store.

You see, if the customer asks for something simple, it doesn't matter who is right or wrong. If it doesn't cost much to save a customer's good will (and to have the customer talk positively about you), go ahead and spend the time, effort, and money. Forget about who is right or wrong or arguing on principle. If you have to fight over the principle of every trivial thing, you belong in a college philosophy department or government bureaucracy. If you're in business and value your customers, don't argue with them.

If the customer demands a new engine, making a settlement is not going to be so easy, but the discussion won't be trivial bickering anymore, either.

The Really Abusive Customer

You've been waiting for me to address this one. You know the case of the clerk or bureaucrat who's been physically attacked, and you want to know what I'll say about defending yourself when talk turns into violence.

Well, I'm realistic enough to say that a thug who's intent on assaulting you is not going to be sweet-talked out of it by somebody who's taken Jerry Wilson's short course in *talk factor* human relations. What you have there is a situation that calls for crime prevention, probably by professionals. But I will offer a few suggestions that should help. They may, at the least, prevent the escalation of a verbal assault into a physical one.

The Don'ts

■ First, do not return a customer's anger with a broadside of your own heated emotions. This kind of talk is unforgivable because it aggravates the negative word-of-mouth situation and puts you at fault for continuing the argument. Watch your words so that you do not give offense, which may be taken as an excuse to resort to violence.

- Second, watch your body language. It can communicate anger or threat more readily than words. If you sneer, lean toward the customer, or clench your fist you are indicating a willingness to escalate the confrontation.

- Third, DO NOT TOUCH. Even a pat on the shoulder can be seen as patronizing. Worse, it can be used as an excuse to retaliate, or the customer might even claim the touch was intended as an assault. I suppose you might say that bar owners employ bouncers to do exactly these things to unruly customers, but that is an example you should not follow.

- Fourth, don't take it personally. The upset customer—even the abusive one—is angry with your company or product. If you can avoid taking offense, you can also avoid injecting your personal feelings into the discussion, making it a personal matter, and sparking another flare-up of hostilities. Finally, don't give in to the temptation to tell any customer to take his business elsewhere. You will gain absolutely nothing, not even lasting satisfaction. Temporarily, you might feel extremely good, but later you will feel embarrassed for allowing yourself to be baited by somebody else's irrational behavior.

Finally, if you've used up all your human relations resources and avoided all the things you should avoid, and the customer is still abusive and threatening, my advice is as follows:

- You can try running through the steps again.
- Send somebody to call for help.
- Get backup.
- Avoid a fight at any cost!

Final Words

When you have followed these steps, you will have done all you can to stop being awful in your business, at least in the eyes of the most vocal talkers, the furious customers who usually deal in negatives. Next you can install a program that removes other, less visible negatives in your company. You can eliminate the in-house talk—generated by you—that says "no" to customers.

SUMMARY OF CHAPTER 6

◆ Rule Six: Word-of-mouth marketing cuts across every organizational and operational division in a company.

◆ The five-breath method of defusing customer fury is the starting point for turning horror stories around.

BREATH 1: Acknowledge that the person is upset.

BREATH 2: Make a sad/glad statement.

BREATH 3: Make a positive statement.

BREATH 4: Ask the magic question.

BREATH 5: Make a settlement.

◆ Do something extra and unexpected. Adding this sixth step generates the first of your positive word-of-mouth marketing stories. You don't have to give away the business, but it's imperative that you make a lasting impression.

◆ Take special precautions in handling the really abusive customer. Avoid confrontations in the first place. Do all you can to prevent them from escalating into violence or abusiveness.

"What you are speaks so loud, I can't hear what you say."

—Ralph Waldo Emerson

7

How To Install a No-Hassle Program

So far, we've talked mainly about the negative aspects of customer satisfaction—really a zone of customer *dissatisfaction*. Within that zone, we've spent most of the discussion on upset and complaining customers, those most likely to start or perpetuate negative word of mouth, and how to diffuse their anger.

The next step on the road to attaining a positive word-of-mouth marketing program addresses all the other customers you serve. If you were to abide faithfully by the advice in the earlier chapters, you'd have traveled a long way. You would not have arrived at what you could call "superb" or "legendary" customer service, but you would have removed many of the negatives. You'd be in the middle region of Figure 7.

This middle region of little talk is an area where you are vulnerable to having your customers lured away.

Negative Word of Mouth		
Awful Service	Good or Adequate Service	Great Service

Figure 7

Most organizations maintain a considerable investment in protecting their territory, telling you all the reasons why you cannot do business with them except on their terms. One time a commercial flight arrangement of mine got fouled up, and I resorted to trying (on a Saturday morning) to charter an airplane. It took 27 phone calls. Everybody wanted to tell me all the things they could not do for me. Not one charter company ever asked me how much money I was willing to spend. For all they knew, I might have been willing to buy the plane. Only on the 28th call did somebody say yes. Your whole business philosophy should be, "We can do things for you."

Let's look at some of the hassles customers have to endure every day.

Just being a customer can be a hassle. Stanley Marcus, formerly of Neiman-Marcus, says it's a myth that customers love to shop. "Pure nonsense. Maybe they used to, but not anymore. Today, customers have more money—and less time—to shop. Shopping no longer has the entertainment value it once had." ("Merchant Prince Stanley Marcus," *Inc.*, June 1987, p. 46)

So imagine what customers expect when . . .

They want to pay by check.

They want to ask a question about a product or service.

They want to special order something—even something as simple as a Big Mac with no pickles.

They just want to return something—no complaint—they just want to return it.

What they expect is a hassle, and for some reason, nowadays they always seem to get it. My favorite example of a more subtle kind of hassle, is the "let me advise you" hassle.

Sam wanted to surprise his wife with a new car for her 70th birthday. To Sam, a really delightful idea of a surprise was to buy her a fire-engine red Trans-Am sports car. Sam had kicked the tires and imagined the excitement of having a car like that just sitting in the driveway—let alone the thrill of driving it home and seeing the look on his wife's face. Then the salesman approached. When he learned the car was intended for a grandmother, he suggested that this sporty red car was for "young drivers." He directed Sam to the more conservative models.

But Sam wanted a fire-engine red Trans-Am. So he bought one—from the Pontiac dealer across town.

Rule Seven: The difference between just operating a business, and operating with no hassle in order to generate positive word of mouth, can be summed up in one word—*attitude*.

If it is true that a customer's perception is everything, then the following is critical to the success of anybody in contact with customers . . . *attitude* is everything.

Call it image, call it appearances, or call it whatever you like. But everything about you and your business proclaims your attitude to every customer who enters.

It can be obvious things like signs, or it can be the lack of signs giving instructions and information about handling complaints or refunds. It can be your cleanliness or that of your employees and your facility. It can be the scent or the temperature of the air in the building. They all can either whisper or shout about your attitude. Attitude is another of those word-of-mouth marketing qualities, a nonverbal form of talk that shouts volumes.

Installing no hassle means taking action to control every factor so the message communicated about your attitude is positive. The message should be, "We welcome you; we welcome your business; we welcome your comments; we even welcome your complaints."

Try these principles for communicating the message of a positive attitude.

The Principles of No Hassle

1.   Remove the negative signs, both active and passive.

2.   Build a sincerely friendly, caring atmosphere.

3.   Make it easy for others to do business with you.

4.   Back up your program with action.

Let's look at each principle.

Remove the Negative Signs

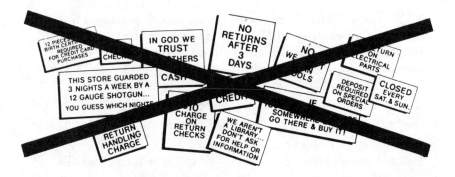

A Chinese proverb says, "Do not use a hatchet to remove a fly from your friend's forehead." It's so obvious a point that at first glance it conjures up a picture of slapstick comedy. No right-thinking person would do to a friend what the proverb advises against. It would seem just as obvious a lesson when applied to customers. Why, then, would somebody in business—somebody who depends on the good will and patronage of customers—hit the customer right between the eyes with negative signs?

I'm speaking literally of signs that say "no"—you've seen them everywhere. Displayed prominently, they tell you all the things the business will not do, and they tell you, the customer, all the things you cannot do in transacting business.

These are examples of some of the actively negative signs, the signs that say no:

No credit.
No checks accepted.
No out-of-state checks accepted.
No returns.
No returns of sale items.
No return on . . . [electrical parts, special orders, you name it]
No soliciting.
No trespassing.

And here are some other ways of saying negative things without using the word "no":

Closed weekends.
Deposit required on special orders.
$15 handling charge on all returned checks. (I've always wondered, how are you going to collect the $15 from a dedicated bad check artist? Seems to me the only people you affect with this kind of policy are those you further embarrass after they've made a checkbook error.)
Beware of dog.

Negative signs do not become more palatable with wise-crackery or humor:

We honor Mastercard, VISA, and American Express—However, we accept only cash.
In God we trust—Others pay CA$H.
This store guarded 3 nights a week by a madman with a shotgun . . . you guess which nights.

These sorts of signs and all the variations imaginable are doing damage to your business. You are blaring a negative attitude in a silent form if you use them. Your word-of-mouth marketing program cannot succeed while you have such roadblocks posted around your establishment. You might as well be standing at the door with a hatchet offering to rid your customers of flies.

Instead, get rid of the negative signs. That's the first step of no hassle. Take them down and destroy them.

I know one hardware store owner whose eyes were opened by no hassle. He looked around and saw the active signs all over expressing no to this and no to that: "No return on plumbing supplies;" "$20 charge on returned checks;" "10% restocking charge on all returned goods." The store actually had a sign that belligerently declared: "If you want help or information about installation . . . the library is down the street."

This owner had just bought the store and inherited all the signs. The signs had been up so long, none of the employees even seemed to notice them. But the owner had read an article I wrote about negative signs, and, suddenly, he saw that every message on his walls was a negative one.

He presided over a sign-burning ceremony and torched the signs in the presence of all his employees. It signaled his intention to them to rid the business of an actively negative attitude. He also told them his company was adopting a no-hassle policy toward every customer.

Naturally, he expected his customers to appreciate the idea of no-hassle, but he received an extraordinary bonus from his employees. They became happier because it was no longer required that they give customers a bad time. When items came back, the employees no longer had to try to extort the 10 percent restocking penalty from reluctant customers.

Take a look at your invoices and advertisements. How many times does "no" appear? Is it on your handbills or your windows? Do these items send a literally negative message? Strike these messages from your printed materials everywhere.

You want your customers to say "yes" emphatically when asked for the buying decision, don't you? Start by changing the atmosphere of your business by saying positive things yourself.

If you don't want to hold a ceremony, at the least you should take down the negative signs at your team meeting, which should include both line and staff people. This is a positive sign, isn't it? It's a message to the employees that no-hassle is being introduced as a matter of policy. You should send the message that your purpose is to install the program, not to debate it. In this way, you'll bring everybody on board. Remember, that's where word-of-mouth marketing starts—aboard your own ship.

Build a Sincerely Friendly, Caring Atmosphere

This requires you to take positive steps. If you are sincerely friendly and caring, the relationship between you and the company's employees will reflect that. If you're an old grouch, you will be transmitting your negativity like electricity through your employees, and will shock the customers unlucky enough to come into contact with your business. If you wish to change your appearance and behavior, that's possible, but you'll have to work at it. The next step will be to ensure that you hire and train employees so they reflect a positive attitude. Naturally, you must inform your customers of your policies on taking checks and other essential matters of doing business, but this can be done without signs that scream negatives.

Don't worry about giving the store away. You may have to face the objections of employees worried about being swamped by customers demanding refunds or exchanges. You'll have to remind them of companies like Sears, which proclaims "satisfaction guaranteed" and runs advertisements promising refunds or exchanges—no embarrassing questions asked. One I particularly admire is a television commercial showing an Oriental couple returning an appliance. Although the Sears employee and the couple cannot speak each other's language, the customer's need is instantly diagnosed and met. As the couple leave the store, the woman remarks to her husband (her words appear in subtitle) about the "nice young man." There are many messages in this ad: "We're friendly to all races and ages of people; the language of sincerity transcends the barriers of spoken language; you don't have to explain to get satisfaction at Sears; Sears wants you to return to its stores, even if it's only to return merchandise; Sears likes you; Sears is sincere; Sears cares."

At seminars I sometimes demonstrate a point by calling a volunteer forward and giving the person a $100 bill. Universally, the recipient smiles—people like to receive money. Then I ask the person to return the money to me. Universally, the smile fades as the money—mine in the first place—is handed back. People hate to give up money, even when it didn't belong to them in the first place.

The point of this demonstration is this—it's a natural inclination of your employees to resent giving refunds to customers. Although the money was not actually theirs in the first place, giving it back is taken to mean a failure of some kind or a loss that's taken personally. You'll have your work cut out for you, but you must instill several characteristics in all your employees who deal with customers. These are the characteristics indispensable for dealing with customers:

- **Friendliness.** This is not the "have a nice day" friendliness, the automatic slogans that slip meaninglessly out of the mouth. No, friendliness is a natural inclination that most people understand, and you should encourage it among your present employees. You should hire friendly people to deal with customers.

- **Helpfulness.** Customers buy because they have needs and wants. Although every sensible business person should first fully understand the importance of making a profit, it follows naturally that to do so requires the fulfillment of the needs and wants of customers. This requires cultivating a sincere desire to help people make their buying decisions.

- **Unflappability.** This means not taking customer complaints personally. This means developing the ability to keep the smile on your face after somebody gives you a $100 bill and then takes it away.

- **Gamesmanship.** Serving others should be viewed as a game without losers. If you and your employees see this game as a win-win proposition, a contest where nobody has to lose, then everything else being suggested in no hassle will be easy to accept. The importance of this last characteristic is stressed by Alan Paison, president of the Customer Satisfaction Division of Walker Research, a company that has capitalized on the emerging importance of measuring customer service and satisfaction. Paison says that especially in the delivery of services, there is an enormous challenge in dealing with customer complaints. To adapt to the situation and deal with it, he says you must make it a game. The object of the game is to win satisfaction. You have to say to yourself, "How much do I have to do to win this game? The only way for me to win is to convince you absolutely that I'm a genuinely concerned, service-oriented person. The only way for me to lose is to fail to win your satisfaction. I'm not going to allow you to think that I can't do it."

Can you actually train employees in the art of friendliness? I believe so. Good attitudes are possible for almost everybody. Paul J. Meyer, of Success Motivation Institute, said, "Attitudes are nothing more than habits of thought . . . and habits can be acquired."

In order to do this, you must first show that you mean it. If you're always grumbling at your people to smile, what chance does the program have? Your customer satisfaction program has no more hope of success than your employee satisfaction program. Nothing is more contagious than a smile. Dale Carnegie suggested the importance of smiling by devoting an entire chapter to it in *How to Win Friends and Influence People*.

Carnegie wrote, "Actions speak louder than words, and a smile says, 'I like you. You make me happy. I am glad to see you.'"

That's an extremely important impression to have your employees make on customers.

Not long ago, I finished a consulting engagement early and went to the airport to try to change flights so that I could arrive home earlier. I approached the "Ticket Change" line, where a matronly lady stood with a scowl on her face. She wore a tag with one of those happy faces and the words, "Hi! I'm Holly." I wanted to say to her, "If you're so happy, why not tell your face?" But I didn't, I just tried for a ticket change. The schedule adjustment couldn't be made, so I decided to check my bags and relax for a while. She refused to check the bag. "You have to go to that line over there," she said, pointing to a hundred people waiting in a line. No matter how much I reasoned, she refused to budge because I had not actually been able to change my ticket. In less time than it took to explain it, she could have checked the baggage. It wasn't that big of an adjustment—after all, I *had* tried to change flights in earnest. Nobody from the other line would have started a riot because she gave me a break. As I walked away, I felt a weird little chill at the back of my neck . . . as if she were smiling after all at the hassle she had given me.

I once concocted a "Smile Training Program" for my employees at a parts store. You may think this stretches the point to an extreme, but I assure you that it worked—it indelibly drove home my commitment to no hassle.

I simply painted a yellow pair of size 12 footprints on the floor in a storage area. Then everybody in the store went on "frown patrol." Every time an employee was caught red-handed (red-faced?) with a frown while handling a return or refund, that employee had to stand on those footprints for a minute and practice smiling.

I spent a few minutes on those footprints myself, and I discovered what made them effective. You see, we're not always conscious of our expressions, and the threat of being banished to those prints made all of us adopt a new self-awareness. The capacity to smile was always there. We just encouraged ourselves to exercise that capacity.

Make It Easy for Others To Do Business with You

Today, accepting every form of customer payment is not optional. Research has proven that a high percentage of check and credit card purchases consists of "plus" business. Many customers won't buy from you—even if you advertise lower prices—if you won't accept the form of payment *they* want to use. It's a hassle for them. You can reduce this hassle to nothing. Here are a few tips on how:

- ■ **Sign up with a check guarantee service.** You can insure checks for one or two percent of the amount. Then you can begin accepting checks from anyone, anywhere, anytime, with no risk.

- ■ **Accept, at the very least, VISA, MasterCard, American Express, and Discover.** If your business lends itself to it, you can also take oil company cards and Diners Club.

- ■ **Boast that you are easy to do business with.** Display decals and credit logos on your vehicles, in every ad, in the yellow pages, on your front door, on counters, in all printed materials (especially invoices), and all around the store. Don't assume that people will assume that you accept these cards. Studies repeatedly show that customers in doubt will not risk embarrassing themselves by asking if you take cards. Many are either too timid or in too great a hurry to ask. They will just go elsewhere until they see the signs that help them use credit.

Use the following words in designing professional signs of your own. Let people know how easy it is to do business with you:

- SURE IT'S EASY TO DO BUSINESS WITH US
- WE ACCEPT . . .
- PERSONAL CHECKS
- (WITH PROPER I.D.)
- VISA
- AMERICAN EXPRESS
- MASTERCARD
- DISCOVER
- CASH, OF COURSE

Guarantee No Hassle

Launch your no-hassle program convincingly with a promise to guarantee not only your product or service, but also your professional delivery of them. You should hire a printer or painter to design a number of signs that will stand in every place you advertise. Print them and place them in every customer order or billing. By doing so, you will be reassuring customers, you will be inviting complaints (which can help you increase profits), and you will be committing your business forever to this policy and to an ongoing promotional campaign. The words (see Figure 8) speak for themselves, and the results will include

---

WE GUARANTEE NO HASSLE
    When you spend your money with us, you are trusting us to provide you with the best in both products and services. We want to earn your continued business, not give you a hassle.
    If you are not completely satisfied with something purchased in our stores —TELL US. We will make it right or refund your money.
    We want your business, and we guarantee you NO HASSLE.
    (Your name and position as guarantor)

Figure 8

the creation of an atmosphere conducive to generating positive word of mouth.

Back Up Your Program with Action

You can take down all your negative signs and put up all the positive signs you want, but if you don't live by your printed words, it won't mean a thing. It won't take long for your customers to see whether you're serious. If you're not—if you still seem unfriendly, and if doing business with you remains difficult—matters will be all the worse. For now, in addition to being seen as negative, you'll be seen as two-faced about it because of the facade of smiling faces and pleasant messages you've posted on your walls and windows.

SUMMARY OF CHAPTER 7

◆ Rule Seven: The difference between just operating a business, and operating with no hassle in order to generate positive word of mouth, can be summed up in one word— *attitude.*

◆ The principles of no hassle create the environment for a positive word-of-mouth marketing program.

1. Remove the negative signs, both active and passive.

2. Build a sincerely friendly, caring atmosphere.

3. Make it easy for others to do business with you.

4. Back up your program with action.

"The proof of the pudding is not in the tasting but in whether people return for a second helping."

—Bob Levoy, Consultant

Nobody Talks about "Good" Service

By now you should realize that the easiest way to launch a negative word-of-mouth marketing campaign is to conduct your business as horribly as possible. I've dedicated the previous chapters to showing you how to shut off the awful talk. That should bring you up to "good" in the category of the critical *talk factor,* service. *But good service isn't good enough!* Take a look at Figure 9. You've moved

Negative Word of Mouth	No Word of Mouth	
Awful Service	**Good or Adequate** Service	**Great Service**

Figure 9

from the shaded area on the left, Awful Service, to the middle, which is Good Service, or merely being adequate.

The trouble is, *nobody talks about adequate service!*

You may think I'm kidding. Do you remember the last time you went to eat at one of those nationally advertised fast food franchises? Did you and your family leave the place raving about the food? Not likely. If anything, your kids may have gotten excited about the toy giveaways, but not the food, unless the food or the service was terrible. When you go to one of those places, you expect the food to be edible, hot, fast, and consistent. If the place meets those standards of adequacy, your expectations are met, and you leave without another thought. Only if your expectations are not met, or if they are exceeded, do you spread the word of mouth about a business. In your own company it follows that if you want to get word of mouth really working for you, you must adopt the following rule:

Rule Eight: Blow your customers away by exceeding their every expectation.

Bob Levoy, president of Professional Practice Consultants of Great Neck, New York, says, "People don't get excited about receiving their regular paychecks. But they do get excited when they get a bonus. The customer who receives a 'bonus' feels the same way, and for the same reason. You have given him something to get excited about."

Levoy also says, "Ask a satisfied customer how he likes a supplier and the customer will say something like, 'Oh, he's okay, I guess. You'll get what you paid for.' Ask the same question of an enthusiastic customer and his reaction will be something like, 'That salesperson is the greatest. He really gives you extra attention and service. Let me tell you what he did for me last week.' If you were looking for a new supplier, whom would you call first?"

Negative Expectations

Too often, the customer walks into a business situation *hoping* somebody will exceed his or her expectations in the delivery of goods and services. Much too often, the customer's hopes are dashed. *Time* magazine did an entire cover story in the February 1987 issue about how badly service has deteriorated in America. There followed a wave of customer service books and articles lamenting the state of service in America and offering tips on how to fix it.

People *expect* to have something go wrong when they shop. I have a friend who's adopted a very extreme posture. He has no hope at all that *anything* will go right.

"Nothing works!" is his philosophy, and he has enough true stories to back up the idea that you should always assume the worst. For instance, he's been shorted a hamburger or an order of fries often enough at the nearest fast-food chain that he never drives away from the take-out window without conducting an audit of his food bags. You'd check the order, too, if you had to take food to his house and face three teenagers in a feeding frenzy over two bags of fries!

A family in our neighborhood moved into a new house to find the normal little glitches and one pretty serious one—the plumber had connected the toilets to the hot water lines.

A customer service representative from a major furniture store told me in my research that an elderly couple ordered a new sofa that collapsed the first time they sat on it. After the piece was repaired, it collapsed again!

You know these stories, too. Hardly anybody who's ordered a new car can escape the trip back to the dealership for at least minor repairs. In this morning's newspaper, I read two stories that supported the "nothing works" philosophy. In one report, a major automobile manufacturer had to recall every one of its new models, priced at $40,000, to repair three defects. In another, toy manufacturers were under fire for advertising items (creating expectations) on Saturday morning television, showing the toys doing things they couldn't do in reality.

You know a hundred stories like the ones I've just detailed. What's wrong here?

Setting Goals and Objectives

I have a theory. The reason most businesses fail to exceed customer expectations of service is because they fail to think from the customer's perspective. They fail to consider what it's like to do business with their organizations.

The second most important reason businesses fail is because they fail to exceed their own expectations of themselves—if (and this is a big if), if they even have any expectations of themselves at all.

Look at this principle in terms of the following diagram, Figure 10, which looks like an archery target. The quality of customer service is arranged in concentric circles from awful to good to great.

Imagine yourself shooting at the target. Obviously, hardly anybody starts out aiming to deliver awful service. The trouble is, too many companies shoot blindly at the target or only aim to deliver good service. The law of averages dictates that even the best company will have incidents where their service falls into the awful category, and on occasion, they'll deliver great service—even if only by accident.

The trouble is, by having no word-of-mouth marketing and customer service goals, or in setting your goals on delivering good service, the chances of falling into the great category depend as much on fate and accident as on anything else.

However, when you set a goal to deliver great service in order to

Figure 10

exceed expectations and to generate positive word of mouth, the chances are good that on your worst days, you fall no lower than into the good category of service. What is the lesson here? It is this: The first step toward exceeding the customer's expectation of your business is to exceed *your own* expectations of your customer service.

You start by setting your goal at the bullseye. You may object to reaching so high—after all, nobody is perfect. Even L. L. Bean and Walt Disney Productions must have disgruntled customers and customer service disasters sometimes. Granted, you are human, and humans make mistakes. But why shouldn't you set high goals for your customer service? Why not shoot for near perfection? You'll agree that you'd never shoot for awful customer service, wouldn't you? It's easy to entertain the possibility of delivering good customer service, isn't it? Why not great? Why not legendary?

To have any chance at all for a viable word-of-mouth marketing program, you must avoid the negative and transcend the enormous area of adequacy that is the curse of most businesses. You must exceed expectations in a substantial way.

Fortunately, the positive side of the woeful state of service in America is that with very little effort you can meet the low expectations of your customers, and just by doing a little extra, you can exceed them.

Do you have written customer service goals? Do you emphasize the delivery of outstanding service with two aims: to get repeat business and to generate word of mouth? Most business people neglect to focus on any customer service objectives at all. Most businesses fail to meet and exceed customer expectations because *they have no goals at all!*

I assure you that simply putting up a sign that reads, "The customer signs your paycheck" in the employee break room, yet failing to set goals, is the same as having no goals at all. I further assure you that you cannot possibly hope to meet or exceed customer expectations, except by accident, if you have not set goals and objectives. So let's do that first, and let's begin by differentiating between goals and objectives. A *goal* is a statement of policy or principle that establishes a company mission in terms of customer service and word-of-mouth marketing. Even a one-person operation should have them.

Objectives are qualitative and quantitative standards by which you measure your own performance. For example, the (admittedly long-winded) goal for a coffee shop owner might be "To provide superb service and great coffee every day, so that our customers will rave about the coffee to others, building our business by word of mouth; to keep our daily customers from trying the competition, and to impress the city magazine so that it will select our coffee in the annual 'Best of the City' awards." One objective you might set to measure your performance would be "To serve every cup of coffee at a temperature no lower than freezing." That's a low expectation of yourself, of course. It would inspire only the lowest expectation in customers, too. Any word of mouth you generated would be negative.

What I'm saying here is that you need very specific goals and objectives with high standards. A set of objectives that define the truly great cup of coffee might be "Coffee must be ground fresh daily from refrigerated beans. It must be served hotter than 150 degrees in pre-heated cups; any pot more than a half hour old must be discarded; the pot must be cleaned and rinsed before every fresh pot is brewed; no customer will be served the last cup of coffee in a pot—it will be discarded and the customer will be served from a fresh, full pot; and at the end of every day white vinegar will be percolated through the coffeemaker to clean it for the next day's operation. Any cup of coffee served without meeting such a standard is considered inadequate and therefore unacceptable."

This definition of the mechanics, with any refinements you could add, might define the perfect cup of coffee. Next, a set of standards might be constructed to define the flourish with which such perfection must be served. For example, you might pour from a silver service set or use whole cream and so on. This would increase the chances for exceeding a customer's expectations and improve the odds for inspiring word of mouth.

Finally, to put the objective into a word-of-mouth marketing context, the server might be given instructions to generate talk. I can think of a number of ways to do this. If the server simply told of the high standards that dictated the preparation of the coffee, the customer could hardly avoid talking about the experience. The server might plant the idea that this would be the greatest cup of coffee in town before the first sip was taken, as a way of calling attention to the drink. You get the idea, don't you?

Forces That Shape Customer Expectations

Before you can possibly hope to exceed customer expectations, you must understand how those expectations are formed. You can start by looking at your customers in a new way. Look at the next one who walks in the door. Is that truly a customer, or is it a client, a champion, or a prospect?

Look at Figure 11. Imagine this man has just entered the neighborhood drug store you own.

Take a look at the circles around the person's head. Those circles show the forces that shape his expectations. Let's examine the forces around our model customer and analyze his expectations.

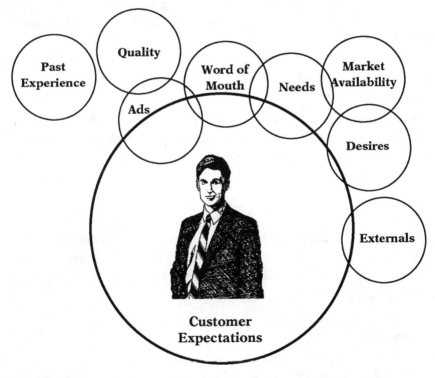

Figure 11

Needs

This customer's needs are simple. His wife's birthday is today. He needs a good gift quickly. You can tell by the large overlap in the diagram that it's a big need. Of course, you can't see that on a real customer, but in most sales situations, you could find out by simply asking, "What do you need?" Let's not talk about selling yet, though.

Desires

This is a small factor in our model's circle. He merely wants to shop close to home.

Ads

You've advertised a special on women's fragrances. That is a concrete factor shaping this man's expectations when he walks into your establishment.

Market Availability

Since there's no overlap with expectations, the model shows it as not being a factor. Nearly every department and drug store sells perfumes, so you don't have this man's market cornered.

Quality

Since there is no difference in quality between what you offer and what the competition sells at the same price, this factor has no bearing on this customer. If you were to add extra value to your perfume products, it might become a factor.

Externals

These are your location, signs, lighting, and appearance. If yours are bright, clean, and lively, he'll have one set of expectations. If you're dingy, stuffy, and dirty, he'll have a different set.

Past Experience

The model shows this customer has not shopped with you before. His expectations are not shaped by any experience with you.

Word of Mouth

In part, this is your reputation. It is shaped not by personal experience, but by a combination of all the other factors. For instance, your ads "talk" about you. Your signs "talk" about you. Your competition spreads rumors. Your employees speak volumes about you by their attitudes, appearances, and their actual words. Your satisfied customers pass along testimonials about your products and services, establishing your word-of-mouth reputation.

At a glance, you might correctly conclude that you've already had countless chances to form the customer's expectations before he's ever arrived at your entrance or picked up a telephone. It's also easy to see that the stronger you have made a word-of-mouth marketing impression, the more likely you'll get this customer's business. Then, depending on how well or badly he is influenced once he's made personal contact with you, he will create his own version of word of mouth and decide whether to give you his business.

Your First and Lasting Impression

You never get a second chance to make a first impression. That's what the shampoo commercial says. I might add a brief note—it pays for that first impression wildly to exceed customer expectations. How are you going to do that?

Let's go back to the model of our customer with the circles as he walks into your business, phones, or reads the mailing you have sent. Remember the circle labeled "past experience"? The moment that customer began to form his first impressions about your externals, the past experience circle began to overlap the customer expectation circle. He began forming perceptions that will become his past experience the second he walks out the door. He's deciding every time another stimulus reaches his senses. If his nose begins to burn from the odor in your store, he's formed a perception. Every instant is another opportunity for another stimulus to affect his decision.

What is he deciding? That's easy. He's deciding whether word of mouth has painted your reputation accurately. He's matching his own perceptions to his expectations. Are you awful? Are you outstanding? He's deciding whether you've met his expectations, whether you've fallen short, whether you're going to blow him away or brush him off.

Are you going to leave that decision to chance? Are you going to let that customer decide all by himself? For Pete's sake, no! You can't afford to. You have to be aware of that hideous gap between what a customer expects and what the customer perceives that he or she has received.

I did *not* say that the problem is the gap between what the customer *expects* and what the customer *receives*. What I said was that the problem is the gap between what the customer expects and what the customer *perceives* he or she has received.

Tom Peters, author of *In Search of Excellence* and other books, flatly declares that with service, there is no reality. There is only perception, and the customer's perception is everything. You put the *talk factor* to work for you when you provide service so outstanding that it becomes legendary—when your service blows them away.

Walker Research of Indianapolis, Indiana, uses a model that describes these five gaps that can occur in service delivery.

■ Gap 1—between what the customer expects and what management perceives the customer wants

Al Paison is president of the customer service division of Indianapolis-based Walker Research, one of the industry leaders in measuring customer satisfaction. Paison says, "If you interview the top ten executives of most American businesses, you're going to find a difference between what they think their customers want and what their customers actually do want."

This gap can have enormous consequences. Senior managers set the strategy and direction of the business. If their perception of what the customer wants is wrong, it's not likely the company and the customer will ever be in synch. The relationship goes even further downhill when company's goals and standards are written without regard for customer expectations.

■ **Gap 2—between what management perceives and the translation of those perceptions into specifications for delivery of goods and service**

Paison says, "If management truly knows what the customers want, they have to translate those perceptions into specifications that work. That's the formalization of the operation. If you do this poorly or inaccurately, you have another opportunity for poor service."

He described one Walker client who had a problem in billing, which can be irritating for any customer. "We were watching billing in a customer satisfaction study. Suddenly customers started becoming unhappy with billings when there hadn't been a problem there before. We found a new manager had come in and had decided to improve billing efficiency by raising the objective from 2,500 bills a day to 3,000. The next thing you know, they're pumping out bad bills and they think they're being successful. But customer satisfaction goes down."

Paison described this as a case where customers want fast, accurate bills. But when the two specifications are at odds with one another, accuracy should always take precedence.

Bridging this gap is a matter of thorough training, setting objectives, and continual monitoring.

■ **Gap 3—between the translation of perceptions into specifications and actual delivery of service**

Having high, accurate specifications means nothing if the specifications aren't met. This is another case where good management must determine what it expects. The aim is to establish reasonable standards that meet or exceed customer expectations, then ensure that the company meets the standards. Of what value is it if a coffee shop insists on great coffee in the operations manual, and the drink is cold and stale in the cup?

■ **Gap 4—between what external communications say that the service will be, and what is actually delivered**

Here is simply a case of Gap 3 amplified. When you tell the world what the standard is, whether you live up to the standard becomes of much greater consequence. Paison says, "Holiday Inn promises you'll be satisfied with the accommodations or the room is free. That's bellying up to the bar with the dollars."

■   **Gap 5—between the perceived delivery of service and what the customer expected to get**

"If you expect the best of us, it's something we'll have to live up to," says news anchor Peter Jennings in a television promotion for ABC's *World News Tonight*.

That's about it. If you're shooting for exceeding customer expectations, you have to exceed what *they* want, not what *you* think they want. Your success depends on their perception of what they've gotten, not what they actually received.

One business where giant Gap 5s often occur is in new automobile warranties. Maybe you've heard of horror stories where owners returned to have repairs made on a new car, only to find that the specific problem is not covered by the warranty.

You've heard of Rolls-Royce Motor Cars, Inc., haven't you? In fact, the term Rolls-Royce is often applied as a superlative to describe other products, as in "This is the Rolls-Royce" of computers, or fountain pens, or toasters.

A couple was motoring across Europe in a Rolls-Royce and broke an axle in the car. They placed a telephone call to the company for repairs. Within an hour, a helicopter landed alongside the road, and several mechanics in white coats replaced the car's axle. Weeks went by and the couple didn't receive a bill, so the man called to ask why none had been received. He was told, "We can't find any record of that, so there is no bill to be sent you. In actuality, though, a Rolls-Royce axle couldn't break."

Most likely, you can't hire a helicopter to perform such miracles. You don't have to. Great customer service usually isn't one big thing, spectacularly done. More often, it's hundreds of little things done well. You don't have to sacrifice thousands of dollars to become legendary in service and gain the attendant positive word of mouth.

One example of such a tiny but effective thing comes from Frank Engler of Van Nuys, California, whose wife took a pair of flat tires to a service station to be repaired. The station owner saw that the valve stems had been removed. He simply replaced the stems, filled the tires, and reinstalled them on the car—for nothing.

The owner insisted on *not* being paid. He said, "Ma'am, the goodwill I will gain and the word-of-mouth advertising you will give me will far surpass the cost of a couple minutes work and twenty-five cents in parts."

Word of mouth. It can come from just one little thing at a time.

Do the Little Things

If you could do 100 little things with every customer, you'd blow every one of them away. I guarantee you'd exceed their expectations and energize the *talk factor*, putting it to work for you. I'm going to share a few gems with you now. Don't be alarmed because they are simple and inexpensive. Just try one of them at a time, then stand back and watch the results they can bring you. By the way, I've devoted all of Chapter 14 to discussing the 100 little things in detail.

- **Launch a "one little thing" program.** Merchants Tire of Manassas, Virginia, has printed a special block on its service forms. Every employee who services an automobile must find one little thing to fix on each car. The item must be repaired free of charge, and the block on the form must be checked. When the customer picks up the automobile, he or she is told of the little freebie. Talk about energizing word of mouth!

- **Win over the family and menagerie.** Keep your eyes open for kids and pets that come in with your customers. Give lollipops to the children and biscuits to the dogs. Get something special for women customers, and get plenty of them. Imagine handing a crimson rose to a man and telling him, "Take this to your favorite woman. She'll love you for your thoughtfulness." It works . . . they *both* will talk about you.

- **Assemble a "goof kit."** In fact, put together several grades of your goof kit. Everybody makes mistakes. If you make a little mistake with a customer, admit it and put a nice pen and memo pad into their order bag. That's goof kit "A." A bigger mistake might warrant goof kit "B," a pair of movie tickets or a gift certificate for a nearby restaurant. A real whopper might warrant goof kit "C," a case of steaks. You decide how badly you want to generate positive word of mouth. You can also arrange this kit according to your word-of-mouth marketing pyramid, instead of by the severity of your mistakes. Using this method, you would give the more valuable gift according to the position somebody occupies on your pyramid. A champion would get goof kit "C," the case of steaks, for example.

■ **A calling card for every employee.** Drivers? Counterpeople? Yes. They're important enough for this tiny investment. They'll be proud to leave their card with every customer and every prospect. They'll use that card with friends and relatives, and your business will have its name in many unexpected places. That card will talk for you! And because you've made them feel important, your employees will be talking about you. Powerful talk it is, too. An added touch on that card should be the hotline number for when problems occur. The last transaction between your employee and the customer should be the employee telling the customer to call if anything should go wrong.

■ **Reach out and touch them.** This might take a bit of work, but set up a call-back system to contact every customer or client after they do business with you. You want to do three things:

1. To find out that there has been no problem with the service or product, or to correct any problems.
2. To tell your customers to come back because you want them to do business with you for the rest of their lives.
3. To tell the customers to tell their friends about you, so they can become customers too. This is blatantly a case of pushing the *talk factor*, isn't it?

■ **Never let the customer feel stupid.** Here's as good a place as any to make an exception to the rule of meeting and exceeding customer expectations. At one time or another, you have probably returned to a store with a gadget that refused to work for you. Somewhere in the back of your mind that nagging voice of insecurity whispered that you'd probably be embarrassed. You'd read the instructions completely and followed them, yet you couldn't get the product to function. So you went back to the store, the voice now murmuring that you were going to be made to feel stupid.

The clerk at the return counter took one look at the item and—with raised eyebrows—said, "Did you engage the flapdoodle before plugging it in?"

You said, "What flapdoodle?"

The clerk's attitude shouted, "See! You dumb jerk, you *are* stupid!"

The voice in the back of your head didn't have to shout about your stupidity any longer, because the clerk's attitude and body language were doing quite a good job of it.

Don't exceed your customers' expectation that they're going to be embarrassed.

Great customer service usually isn't one big thing spectacularly done. More often, it's hundreds of little things done well.

I can almost imagine what some will say about these suggestions. Some of the ideas cost a little money. Others require a little effort. That's absolutely true. To become legendary in service so you can stimulate positive word of mouth will require something more than the ordinary. But remember this fact about word-of-mouth marketing—it requires very little effort and money to be plain old ordinary and have nobody talk about you, and it takes *no* effort to be awful—when people are saying all the wrong things. Remember the word-of-mouth continuum, shown again in Figure 12.

How do you know how well you're doing? The best source of

Negative Word of Mouth	No Word of Mouth	Positive Word of Mouth
Awful Service	Good or Adequate Service	Great Service

Figure 12

information is the customer who had a complaint or problem with your product or service. Seeking complaints is the topic of the next chapter.

SUMMARY OF CHAPTER 8

◆ Rule Eight: Blow your customers away by exceeding their every expectation.

◆ Customers often walk into a business with negative expectations.

◆ Set service goals that include word-of-mouth considerations. Goals are statements of policy or principle that establish a company mission.

◆ Set objectives that include word-of-mouth considerations. These are the standards by which you measure your own performance. Remember, you must set high standards to achieve excellence.

◆ Recognize the forces that shape customer expectations. Remember how needs, desires, ads, competition, quality, experience, past experience, market availability, externals, and word of mouth affect the customer.

◆ You must create a good first impression. The problem in doing this is often the gap between what the customer expects and what the customer *perceives* he or she has received.

◆ Five gaps exist that threaten the delivery of service. These must be overcome continually to preserve positive word of mouth.

◆ Exceeding expectations is often a matter of consistently doing the little things properly.

"Those who enter to buy, support me. Those who come to flatter, please me. Those who complain teach me how I may please others so that more will come. Only those hurt me who are displeased but do not complain. They refuse me permission to correct my errors and improve my service."

—Marshall Field

9

Seek Those Invaluable Complaints

In my life, I have bought several homes, a dozen new automobiles, been around the world, rented hundreds of cars, borrowed money from several financial institutions—all major transactions, but I can count on the fingers of one hand the number of times I have been asked whether the service was really adequate.

When were you last asked, "How did we handle your purchase?" "How comfortable did we make you feel during the loan transaction?" "Is there anything we could have done to make this deal go more smoothly for you?" Businesses just don't ask. Most of the time, I (like most of you) didn't feel it was my place to tell these businesses how they might have improved—if they didn't care to ask, why should I have volunteered an opinion?

This chapter is about those who don't talk to you. We've already discussed the very vocal groups, the complainers. If there's a guiding principle on the subject of dealing with the complainers, it could be summarized in this way: *Stop everything and fix the problem.* With those who complain, it is essential to correct their problems so horror stories do not dominate the word-of-mouth about your company. Now is the time to listen to those who don't usually talk to us. While reading this chapter, keep in mind this rule:

> **Rule Nine: Bellow or beg, if you must, but at all costs, let your customers, clients, and champions know you want their complaints.**

The Silent 96 Percent

Every business *needs* complaints. You should thank your customers when they complain because a complaint is one of the most valuable forms of word of mouth.

Why should you thank customers who complain? Because complaints give you information, complaints help you improve your product or service, and, finally, complaints give you the opportunity to save a customer who might be on the way to your competitor. Important as it is to deal with furious customers who complain angrily to you, they represent only 4 percent of all unhappy customers. No wonder you should spend so much time and effort with customers who complain. They're the ones who could give you valuable feedback!

A return customer is in the minority. Studies show that most dissatisfied customers don't talk to you; they don't bother telling you about their problem. They simply leave your business or your product for another. Pay serious attention to the "silent 96 percent."

According to the White House Office of Consumer Affairs, the typical business doesn't hear a peep from 96 percent of the customers who are unhappy with goods or services they receive. That's right: A whopping 96 percent of the customers who are unhappy with your goods or services never complain!

What could be worse than that? you might ask. I'll tell you what could be worse than having the majority of dissatisfied customers never talking to you: The same White House study revealed that 91 percent of dissatisfied customers will never again buy from the company with which they are dissatisfied. Think about that: Fully 91 percent of dissatisfied customers take their business elsewhere. This means they will be taking their negative word of mouth about you elsewhere too.

Even more striking is the fact that customers who do complain (whether they get a satisfactory response or not) are more likely to be loyal customers than those who do not complain at all.

From this information, you should leap to the conclusion that you must find some way to measure customer satisfaction so you can provide the best service possible to the invisible hordes who might otherwise be deserting your company in droves. That's why you must do your best to invite complaints.

Lets start by dealing with the reality of those customers who have complaints but never express them to the business. Remember the crucial statistic: 96 percent of your dissatisfied customers do not complain to business representatives.

Why not?

- **They believe it's not worth the time or trouble.**
- **They don't know how to register a complaint.**
- **They believe complaining will be useless because business people don't care about them or their complaints.**

A Small Business Administration study showed this typical distribution of 100 customers lost to a business:

- One will die.
- Three will move away.

- Five will do business with friends or relatives.

- Nine will find better prices elsewhere.

- Another 14 will have unresolved complaints that drive them away.

- The huge majority, 68, will leave because they see or perceive indifference or a poor attitude at the business.

The first three categories of lost customers are beyond your control. Taken together, the last two categories are of the utmost importance to you, assuming that your pricing and quality are comparable to what your competitors deliver.

Fully 82 percent of all lost customers can be attributed to either poor performance or bad attitude. What a striking statistic!

This statistic, reflecting 82 percent of all lost customers—those who can reasonably be assumed to be at the negative end of the customer satisfaction scale—is the reason for that no-hassle program, which you should install in your business immediately.

Why are these people so important? Because all the people in those last two categories can be influenced. You can't stop that person in the first category from dying, and you probably can't save customers in the second category by persuading them not to move. You can't be best friends or relatives (thank goodness) to everybody. Although you don't dare underprice all your products and services, remember that some people will actually pay higher prices if they perceive that they'll be receiving superior service. Even if you did influence all the customers in those categories, you'd be influencing only 18 percent of all lost customers.

However, you *can* do a better job of handling complaints that do come in, and you can make your complaint procedures so painless that people will not be afraid to bring things to your attention. Complaint handling can pay its own way and then some. In retailing, complaint handling departments have been shown to pay up to 400 percent back to their companies. In automotive services, one government report showed paybacks of 100 percent-plus.

The Nuts and Bolts of Handling Complaints

The idea behind making it easy to complain is simply to reduce frustration for customers and to lessen the number of dissatisfied people who don't complain—but take their business elsewhere.

Allow me to simplify these steps into their briefest form:

- First, draft your "we welcome your complaints" message.

- Second, send your message, using one of four relatively easy and inexpensive methods.

- Third, take those extra steps that distinguish the professionals from the amateurs.

Your customers are the people on your mailing lists and anybody else in the universe you want to patronize your business, come into your restaurant, buy the clothes you sell, and so on. You want to send them a message.

Your "We Welcome Your Complaints" Message

Simply use this format to draft the content of that message. Keep it simple, direct, and conversational. Just fill in the blanks here.

- **Advise your customers that you're eager to hear from them.** Tell them you want to hear *immediately* when something goes wrong. This lessens the chance of unfavorable word of mouth. If you wish, use these very words:

  We welcome your complaints. If you are displeased or dissatisfied in any way with our products or services, please help us to improve . . . tell us what went wrong, and tell us immediately so we can immediately begin fixing it. (Add any other words you feel obliged to use in your message.)

■   **Tell people where to complain.** For example, use words like these: "Please ask for our manager—her name is _____." Or, "Call our hotline number, 555-1234." Or, "Just take one of our postage-free suggestion cards and mail it back to us with a description of the problem you've experienced."

■   **Tell people how to complain.** Tell them what information they need, to whom they should speak, what phone numbers to use, and so on. As always, keep it simple. Just solicit enough information for an initial contact. Later, you can make a personal contact and uncover other, necessary details. You want this initial contact to be so easy that the most timid of customers won't be put off by something they perceive as "red tape."

■   **Right up front, tell people what your limits are.** State your conditions of sale, warranty restrictions, your "fine print" message, if you have one. Tell them your complaint handlers can only do so much, if that is so. Caution: You can overdo the "fine print." I suggest you do no more than absolutely necessary. You don't want people to feel they're being treated like crooks. For example: "Because we value your business, we want you to know this merchandise is marked so low because it has minor, often undetectable, flaws." Or, "This item has been previously owned. As such, the manufacturer's warranty is limited to 30 days."

Once you've stated the essential points of your message, write those points down in the clearest, most unequivocal language possible—plain English. Then, when you're satisfied with the way it reads, prepare to send it.

Four Methods To Send Your Message

■   **Put it in every routine mailing.** Use billing statements and catalogs to get the message out, whether you send an extra flyer inside your mass mailing envelope or actually use a portion of the printed text. In every advertising campaign, make certain your complaint-welcoming message is featured. For example, Quill Corporation includes a pre-authorized return form in every shipment of goods you order from the company.

I'm not talking about fine print, either. Broadcast your message as boldly as if you were throwing open your windows and shouting it into the street. Imagine the attention that would get! Attention is exactly what you want for your message. The more attention it receives, the more likely you will receive positive word of mouth.

You could even use a separate mailing to announce your campaign. Do not underestimate the potential or the necessity of this effort.

Have labels or stickers or envelopes printed with the message: ATTENTION MANAGEMENT—Complaint—Special Handling, Please. Send them in all your mailings. Tell your customers to use your special envelopes or to place your stickers on their envelopes when sending a complaint back to the company. Tell them mail complaints received with such labels are given special attention and that every complaint receives immediate attention. Tell them that every response is reviewed by a company officer. You must mean it. Your customers will sense it soon enough if you're being phony and then they will be gone for good.

Have a few of these printed in the form of a sticker or a trial batch of envelopes that will accompany your orders:

President
(Your firm's address)
IMMEDIATE ATTENTION!!
SPECIAL HANDLING—CUSTOMER
   CORRESPONDENCE!!

■ **Put up signs where people buy.** Make them big and bold and blunt. Tell people either to use a written complaint form, to ask for a manager, or to ask to talk to customer service representatives. Post the phone number where complaints are taken. Have fliers printed so people can take them. Put the information on order forms and vouchers, tickets, tags, checks, and receipts. Put these signs on every wall and on both sides of the doors so people see them coming and going. Your customers must know that you absolutely will *not* compromise in your urgency in soliciting complaints. Incidentally, don't make claims you can't live up to. Once, at a fast-food restaurant, I got lousy service. Next to the service window was a sign that told me I could call the president directly, so I did. The woman who answered had no idea what to do. Don't put up the plaques unless you have a system to deal with the calls.

- **Put the information on your product label.** Tell people what your hotline number is, preferably a toll-free "1-800" number if you do business with customers who don't live in your calling area.

- **Put the message in your warranty and user's manual.** Print it boldly—on the front or back cover.

There they are, the simple, inexpensive steps to get your message out. If you follow these steps and stand behind your promises, avoiding exaggerations and outright lies, give yourself a "C" average in the subject.

Here's as good a place as any to discuss a couple of obvious objections that you might be considering. You might be asking, "For Pete's sake, what if I start getting hundreds of complaints every day? Won't I be swamped? Isn't there a risk I'll go under?"

Do you remember those statistics I gave you earlier? You *don't* have problems when your customers are talking to you in droves. *You have major, unreconcilable problems when your customers stay silent, then leave you in droves.*

If you get hundreds of complaints, rejoice! Even if you are unable to satisfy all those complaints, those customers would be more likely to stay with you than the silent majority. Reliable studies have proven this in business after business.

The second part of my answer to your questions is this: Yes, you do have to take the advice of the Boy Scouts. You must be prepared. My advice is to design your program one step at a time. Stay flexible. Don't get lost in the planning of a complicated program or in trying to execute the entire concept in a single stroke.

An Advanced Program of Word-of-Mouth Marketing

Take Your Message to Your Community

This will distinguish the professionals from the amateur. Let people know you want to hear of complaints. Take the message to public assistance departments, consumer groups, counseling services, and welfare agencies. Go to the Chamber of Commerce, Better Business Bureau, and any of your city, county, and state agencies who are even remotely concerned with businesses like yours. These agencies devote a good part of their resources to helping people and providing information.

What you will be doing is telling them that any complaint about your products or services is immediately welcome. You will give them a fistful of your handbills or instructions on submitting a complaint. Although only a minority of consumers begin their complaint process by visiting one of these agencies, enough of them do to make your contact worthwhile.

Besides, the agencies all too often encounter resistance and defensiveness from those amateurs in business who don't understand the dollars-and-cents value of welcoming complaints. For them it will be a refreshing change of pace. They'll be so impressed, they'll be eager to help people by telling them of your program. They will gladly spread the word of mouth about you.

If your community provides a "Welcome Wagon" program, contact it. Help them acquaint newcomers to the city with at least one very professional business that not only advertises through Welcome Wagon, but also goes out of its way to seek complaints.

Often, newspapers, radio stations, and television stations feature some sort of "Help Line" that champions consumer complaints. Contact the Help Line people—every single one of them. Do not overlook smaller stations and publications. Let these helpers know you're going to help them help if there's ever a complaint about your product or service. An additional benefit to this contact might mean you never show up on the tube as one of those defensive boobs who has to try to explain why he refused a $2 refund to an impoverished handicapped child.

Finally, contact all the welfare agencies by mail or in person. Let them know you want to help their clients immediately if there's ever a problem with your business. Ask them to get in touch at the first sign of trouble so you can clear up misunderstandings and provide satisfaction to anybody dissatisfied with you.

Naturally, there's always the chance you will simply dazzle the people in these agencies. You might never receive a single complaint, but you will have earned a lot of good will. You see, all the people in each of these categories are influential. They meet and talk to many of your potential customers. If any of their clients should ever ask for a reference in making a buying decision, you will immediately come to mind as somebody who seems more than fair and willing to go beyond the promises you make in your ads. Even if they're prohibited from making a specific recommendation about where to buy, they will certainly indicate that you are one business person who will answer a complaint. You've got word of mouth working for you in a systematic way now.

Let me be clear about one thing: You're not visiting these agencies or sending them your "we welcome your complaints" message from some underhanded motive. You're doing it because you truly want to know if people have problems with the things you've sold them.

Start a Speaker's Program

Your speaker's program should reach out to public groups—social, religious, business, and fraternal. Become a speaker yourself, offering to talk to these groups about an area where you are something of an expert. Yes, you *are* an expert. You have a business on the way to greatness. You sell goods or services that you know and understand better than any of your competitors. You share a hobby with some club or group. You have special knowledge about customer service and word-of-mouth marketing. You have something worthwhile to share with others and part of that sharing is giving information about your incredible "we welcome your complaint" program. Although the numbers who get the message are small, they are usually opinion leaders in some section of their communities.

Please be cautioned: do this professionally. Be well prepared and rehearsed, even if you must hire professional help to help you write your message or to lend your delivery a bit of polish. Yes, it takes effort, but it's worth it if it helps broadcast your message.

If you can't find the enthusiasm to do this right, don't do it at all. Better to avoid any impression of half-heartedness in anything you do. There's too great a risk that a shoddy speech will give the impression your business and your sincerity and your complaint-welcoming program are in doubt as well. Don't spread negative word of mouth with your own mouth.

Put Your Message in the Mass Media

Make use of billboards, newspapers and magazines, radio and television. If you do this, be prepared to handle a sudden increase in the number of complaints. But remember the statistics we've already quoted you—people who complain tend to be more loyal customers than those who stay quiet, *even when they don't get a satisfactory response.*

You might want to modify your existing ads to include prominent positioning of the "we welcome your complaints" message. You could include testimonials from impressed customers who have experienced firsthand your commitment to soliciting complaints and solving problems. You also might want to devote part of your ad budget strictly to informing the public and your customers about your sweeping, nononsense plan to attract and resolve complaints.

As I've discussed earlier, I don't recommend blowing the next fiscal year's budget on this step. Better to ease into the use of mass-media methods. However, there's no doubting your sincerity when you do spend money just to tell people how much better your service will be than your competitor's.

Pick Up the Telephone and Talk to Your Customers

You can start simply—with today's customer list if you like. You merely dial the numbers and speak to your customers. Ask if they've had any complaints with your business, church, association, practice, department, or whatever. If they tell you they love you, you have no problem. You smile with your voice and thank them for their patronage.

When they have a complaint, you take immediate action to solve it. Just asking customers how they could be satisfied isn't enough. Certainly, ask them what would make them happy if you like. Better yet, tell them you're sending somebody out to pick up an item that requires repair. Tell them you'll have an exchange item or a refund in the mail immediately—by overnight express, if you really want to excel at this game. Then tell your customers you'll pick up or pay the return freight on the items coming back. Then, as a gesture of your dedication, offer a bonus or discount on the next purchase. Put this customer's name on a priority list someplace so every order or purchase in the future will trigger a tickler system that makes you recheck the quality of service. A customer with a complaint—even a complaint in the past—is now a VIP with your business. That customer is more loyal to you now than almost anybody in your whole clientele who never complained, so you treat him or her with extra respect, admiration, and urgency.

You think I'm crazy? Let me explain. You pay good money to establish new customers and clients—your ads, promotions, give-aways, and samples, yet you expect only a percentage of everyone you contact to give your company a try. What's so crazy about spending a few well-targeted dollars on a customer you already have, somebody who will stay with you forever if you nurture the relationship? What's so crazy about a pro-active word-of-mouth marketing program that will pay off just as surely as your advertising buys?

If you don't have a customer list, it's too late to be miserable about past mistakes. Start one today, using those telephone numbers and names on all the credit cards and credit purchases. Take today's receipts, start your list on 3 x 5 cards, and alphabetize as you go along. Start calling. Beginning tomorrow, start a contest and run it for a week or give something away in a drawing. Then take all the entry slips (which were on 3 x 5 cards, by the way) and alphabetize them. *Now* you have a list. Put out a spiral notebook on your counter next to the registers, and set up a sign advising people that they can get on your mailing list for preferred customers just by writing down their addresses and phone numbers. A local radio station in my hometown has asked listeners to send in a Christmas card that includes a wish for a gift. The station is going to grant some of those Christmas wishes, and, not incidentally, is going to build its mailing list at very little expense. Try some of these ideas. Set up a small giveaway station in your place of business, one that especially caters to children with balloons, a clown, or goodies. Then, as the children are being entertained, tell the parents you'd like permission to call or write to see if there have been any complaints with your business. Take names and numbers for your list.

When anybody calls, ask for names and numbers to return the call with product or service information. If you intend to use this list for advertising, fine, but also tell your customers you care about their satisfaction and mean it.

Give coupons away with the only condition for use being that a customer must put down his or her name and number. Then, each day, call the numbers of the customers who used the coupons and find out whether they received all they paid for in doing business with you.

Is this all too much trouble for you? Fine. People can easily be adequate if they really insist. If you want to transcend adequacy, you're going to have to reach a little. To achieve legendary status, you'll have to reach a lot.

SUMMARY OF CHAPTER 9

♦   Rule Nine: Bellow or beg, if you must, but at all costs, let your customers, clients, and champions know you want their complaints.

♦   Remember that 96 percent of the customers who are unhappy with your goods or services *never* complain! In addition, 91 percent of dissatisfied customers simply take their business elsewhere, and 82 percent of all lost customers can be attributed to either poor performance or bad attitude.

◆ Draft a "we welcome your complaints" message. Tell people you want complaints and tell them how and where to complain.

◆ Send your message using four relatively easy and inexpensive methods.

  • Use all mailings to get the message out.

  • Put up signs at the point of purchase.

  • Put information on your warranties and manuals.

◆ Take advanced steps that distinguish the pros from the amateurs. Take your word-of-mouth marketing message about soliciting complaints to the media and to public agencies.

◆ Develop and lengthen your existing customer lists. Find ways to contact your customers to solicit their feedback about your business, thereby adding powerful fuel to your word-of-mouth marketing campaign.

> "If I put a person into a job and he or she does not perform, I have made a mistake. I have no business blaming that person, no business invoking the 'Peter Principle,' no business complaining. I have made a mistake."
>
> —Peter Drucker in *Marriott's PORTFOLIO*, Fall 1986

10

Word-of-Mouth Marketing Begins with Motivating Your People

Is yours one of those businesses where the first contact between your employees and customers or prospects is a memorable one? If the answer is yes, I offer my reluctant congratulations.

The reluctant part comes from finding too many companies memorable because of employees like "Old Lady Sunshine." Old Lady Sunshine is an ironic label I've put on a certain kind of person I sometimes have to do business with. She seems *old* because of her fixed scowl. I doubt she's a *lady* because I've never known ladies as grumpy as she is. One thing for sure, *she certainly isn't sunshine.* She's like the Grinch or Murky Dismal from one of those children's cartoons. She's misery personified, and her chief function in life appears to be making others feel miserable, too.

When you walk into the restaurant where she works, you have to wait . . . not to be served, necessarily, but just to be noticed! Then she looks you over with disdain before speaking to you. When she does talk, you know you're boring her. She probably won't say more than, "Yeah?" unless she's feeling talkative, in which case you'll get, "What do you need?" At her most polite, she'll ask, "Help you with something?" You're wasting her time. "Hurry up and spend your money and get out of my face"—that's the "silent signal" she sends.

That's why she's so memorable. If you have one like her (or *him,* because plenty of Old *Man* Sunshines exist) in your business, you can bet word of mouth is working against you.

What should you do about people like Old Lady Sunshine? You can go ahead and fire her. That might solve your problem. However, chances are that it will do you no good. Chances are that you have more Sunshines waiting in the wings. Chances are that the person you hire will turn into one.

"How can this be?" you might ask.

Simple. *You* could be at fault. You could be cultivating the negative attitude that results in unpleasant customer encounters. In turn, your employees, who reflect that attitude, are generating unfavorable impressions and negative word of mouth.

Rule Ten: Catch your employees generating positive word of mouth and reward them for it.

How? It's all a matter of motivational adjustments, starting with yours. To turn your employees into *winners,* start by filling your manager's bag with all types of rewards. Then begin passing out the rewards.

Praise

The first item in the manager's bag of rewards is praise. "The last time many people heard applause was at their high school graduation," stated Mary Kay Ash of Mary Kay Cosmetics in *Mary Kay on People Management.*

Everybody loves applause. My wife suggests that Mary Kay might have been wrong in that quotation. It may have been longer for many people, particularly those who didn't graduate from high school.

Well, the essence of adjusting employees' motivation is simply to compliment them when their performance or behavior is exceptional, especially in areas of customer service, the critical factor in developing positive word of mouth. The expression of a compliment or praise may seem very simple. Use a sentence such as: "Thanks, you did a great job of helping Charlie out during the rush, Alice. Your customers left here talking about us. Because of you, I know they'll be back." Or, "You saved my life by coming in early to help with that report for our clients, Don, and I appreciate it. The clients will spread good stories about us through word-of-mouth marketing."

Actually, praising is not as simple as it seems. It comes easily, yes, but not necessarily simply. Follow these steps to making your own positive sunshine:

The 10 Commandments of Complimenting

- **Praise the behavior you want to reinforce.** The behavior that is reinforced will be behavior that is repeated. State your company and customer service goals and objectives. Set standards in your training program. Everybody should know what's expected. When results are achieved, and especially when goals are exceeded, it's up to you to applaud.

- **Avoid plastic remarks.** It's just as important you do not try to scatter praise into every corner of your company. When you praise mediocrity, you'll just be reinforcing the behavior that produced the mediocrity in the first place. If you don't mean the compliment from your heart (warmly, genuinely, and sincerely), keep it to yourself. Nothing is more insulting than faint praise.

- **Be specific in your compliment.** As in the examples above, tell exactly what qualities you admired in the performance. "You've done a nice job this past quarter, John," is perfunctory. It's also vague. How is John to know precisely what behavior is *really* appreciated? Believe me, if he does know, he'll repeat it as often as the rewards of sincere compliments keep coming. "I really liked the way you won over that angry customer today, Phil. I notice you've done that a lot lately."

- **Reward people with immediate compliments.** Do this at the first opportunity after the excellent behavior is observed. Just as punishment loses its effect when administered much later, so does a reward. When possible, praise people on the spot. Never save up either your punishments or your rewards for performance appraisal time. Give sincere compliments all day, every day.

- **When possible, make it a public compliment.** This doesn't necessarily mean pomp and ceremony, but it's often nice to give a simple compliment in the presence of other workers. In the first place, it will boost the employee in the eyes of others and give a vote of confidence to his or her self-esteem. In addition, other workers will notice how you pay recognition. They will then try to meet and exceed your standards in the same way.

- **Make it personal.** Use the person's name, adding to the friendly, comfortable touch you've established.

- **Add an "I-message."** A simple "I appreciate it" tells how you feel about the behavior or performance. Your employees *want* to do well, and they want to please their superiors. There's not the slightest suggestion here that they want to lick your boots. Rather, it's a natural inclination of people to want to please others. You should let them know when they've succeeded with you.

- **Open your eyes.** Look around you and you'll see exceptional performance everywhere, things that people have silently been doing well all along. You'll notice those who always bring their achievements to your attention, of course, but you also see a group of employees simply waiting to be turned into winners!

- **Put it in writing.** This is not to complicate the issue or to suggest you delay giving instant compliments. But you can easily send a note to follow up. You can also write letters of commendation, give certificates, or attach notes to bonuses. You should also collect reminders of compliments for your employees, putting them in a file for performance appraisal time, when you'll repeat your praise in one of the most important forms—in the personnel jacket.

- **Sort out the "buts," "howevers," and "excepts."** Never cheapen a great compliment with some kind of editorial comment, intentionally or otherwise. "Thanks, Wanda, you were magnificent in getting that woman's child to stop crying while she bought our shoes . . . but why didn't you sell a pair for the child, too?" This kind of remark is just about the worst thing you can do. It may be meant as a legitimate suggestion about the practice of "bumping" the customer into an additional sale, but save that item for training or counseling or the meeting later. Give the compliment all by itself so it doesn't get cheapened with the postscript. The compliment pumps up a person's ego instantly. The added comment—no matter how sincere or well-intentioned—becomes more devastating because the pumped-up ego is deflated with a loud bang.

Performance Appraisals

Here's a device in the manager's bag of motivators—the annual review of performance. It's a way of motivating people by putting your praise in writing. The appraisal has many supporters and just as many detractors. I'm in both camps. If the appraisal is used to reward superior performance, especially in the area of customer service, I'm for it. If it is used to bring up problems or counseling on negative traits, I'm against it. Period.

My position is that performance appraisal is a continual process, not a periodic event. You should get in the habit of constantly rewarding productive behavior and correcting poor performance by training, counseling, or example, every single day. There should *never* be an issue brought up at a periodic review that surprises anybody.

If you have adopted the periodic appraisal as a management tool, never write anything negative in it and never bring up areas for correction before the next report. If you want to correct performance, do it when the poor performance occurs or build the correction modification into training. If you want to write remarks about inadequacies, store them in a separate file, a termination file. That's right, termination file—if you put anything negative about employee behavior in writing, you've started on the road to termination. You will be signaling your intention to collect bad news and eventually use it to fire somebody, and as long as the employee knows this, he or she will probably be feeling an inclination to quit before you ever have the chance to complete that file.

In the same spirit, always bring out your biggest guns armed with your most powerful compliments on the performance appraisal. This doesn't mean you have to award everybody the very highest rating in every block of the report (it doesn't mean you can't, though). Use the periodic report to recap all the compliments you've given during the year—in short, do your rewarding and correcting every day but save up only the good stuff. A final word of advice comes from Lee Iacocca, who once said, "If you want to give a man credit, put it in writing. If you want to give him hell, do it on the phone."

Never, never, ever rationalize a less than perfect report by saying, "Nobody is perfect so I knocked you down in this area," or "I never got this high a report myself, so . . . " What a cheap shot! This one is a giant leap down the road toward termination—the quitting kind. Once after a seminar on appraisals, a woman approached me to talk about something she couldn't find the courage to bring up in the open session. She told me about the manager who said he couldn't find anything wrong so he'd been forced to rate her "outstanding" in every category.

"Nobody is capable of doing a perfect job, so next time I'll certainly find some faults in you," he told her. That was no appraisal—that was a time bomb! It's bad enough the guy was an insensitive jerk—just by repeating this story, the woman began to weep. But this boss was a *stupid* jerk. If you find somebody who defeats your best efforts to find fault, is it wise to insult her, bring her to tears, and start her on the road to termination? No! Never diminish the spotlight that shines on your winners. Instead, energize the brightness of that light.

Couple the superlative performance appraisal with some kind of tangible reward, such as an afternoon off, the periodic bonus, or a prize. Give the positive appraisal some meaning by allowing your rated employee to float out of your office on cloud nine.

Permit your employees to write a performance appraisal on you! See how these shoes feel by trying them on yourself. It's not good enough to say your boss already writes one on you. Get your own perspective into shape by seeing how you look on the other side of the paper. Allow these to be anonymous and ask people to be as sincere and compassionate as you are! Be ready to have your eyes opened. Take seriously the results, and even the insults. Prepare to modify your own performance, behavior, and appraisal policy. If you've demonstrated a tendency to catch your people being good, you'll find they've caught you at it, too.

Time

I've become a real nut on managing my personal and professional time. I've also become very respectful of the time of others. In my opinion, you really reward people when you don't waste their time.

The greatest time-waster bosses impose on their employees is the meeting. Don't hold a meeting just to spout opinion or information. Use memos for this. Better yet, host a cocktail party or picnic at your own expense when you want to bore people a little less painfully. They'll be more tolerant of your pontification, more receptive of your hot air if you're plying them with food and drink. Use short, pithy personal memos in place of meetings every time you can.

Promotions

You may be thinking it's about time we started talking about raises and promotions as motivators. True, these are the traditional concerns. They are down here at the bottom of my list for a very practical reason: Not every employee thinks money and promotion are the most important rewards in working for you.

What's more, promotions and raises are so often mishandled that they create a great deal of unrest in a company. How many times have you heard a statement such as, "I should have had that promotion ahead of Gene." Sometimes that kind of remark can be written off as sour grapes, but make sure your promotions truly reward and motivate people rather than upsetting them. Run down this little checklist of how to promote promotions peacefully:

■ **Define the system so everybody understands it.** Establish your ladder of promotions so everybody understands the title, salary, and responsibilities on each rung. Ensure that everybody knows the qualifications and standards for the job in advance—so your men and women may strive for promotions if they want them.

■ **Define it a second time.** This isn't a redundancy. Just writing a job description and prerequisites isn't going to cut it. Now you must get down to specifics. If you list 10 qualifications for a job, list them in order of priority. List those that are absolutely mandatory and indicate if waivers will be considered for the others. Tell your people if time in the company is more important than a college degree or training certificate. That way you won't have misunderstandings from those who aren't selected for promotion, and you will be less likely to have simple misunderstandings grow into grievances.

■ **When a promotion will be available, ensure that everybody qualified knows about it.** If you're not open and fair about these things, you're likely to reward the person promoted and reap a ton of resentment from those who didn't know about it.

■ **Survey all those eligible for promotion to ask whether they want the promotion, if it should be offered to them.** People don't always want new responsibilities. If they're happy where they are, don't make them miserable with a well-intentioned, well-deserved, but unwanted reward. In this instance, it becomes a penalty.

■ **At promotion time, personally inform those who didn't make it.** You owe people who didn't get selected the benefit of hearing your reasoning. You must indicate to them that another person's reward doesn't automatically mean a penalty to them. This is a tough area for managers to handle because it's difficult to put a positive twist to discouraging news. At least, I suggest leveling with the disappointed employees, telling them the realistic chances for a future promotion. You'll want them to accept reality now instead of holding out a false hope you know will simply be dashed later.

■ **Train your people for the next higher job.** Once they master their present positions, they'll be ready to move up your ladder.

Money

It's no accident that salary, earnings, compensation—whatever you call it—is well down this list. Money is important to most people, but not all *that* important as a reward. It's safe to say that most people have a comfort zone in salary, a range that fits them comfortably. Anything below that range of dollars they consider an insult to accept for their work. These are the people who have signs in and around their desks like this one: "I work for money . . . if you want loyalty, hire a dog." Above that range, they strive to achieve for the future, or they simply accept they'll never make much beyond the salary comfort zone. Once they're in their safe, comfortable range, other really important factors begin to play a role on the job. Most employees don't see money as a reward . . . because they contribute time, effort, and expertise, they see their basic compensation as a right. In fact, it *is* a right.

If you want to capitalize on compensation more as a reward than a right, you can. Try some of these suggestions for salary as a reward:

- **Use longevity raises sparingly and don't treat cost-of-living raises as rewards.** Don't pay people increases merely because they managed to keep working for another year. If you pay cost-of-living allowances or raises, their very nature categorizes them as entitlements, not rewards.

- **Tie raises to performance appraisals.** When you say those nice things about your people, back it up with a raise. What a perfect way to tie a reward to praise and thus make it more meaningful.

- **Whenever possible, find a bonus formula that reflects a sharing of the profits.** This type of compensation keeps a person conscious that daily success will be rewarded if the whole team wins.

- **Negotiate alternatives to pay raises.** To some people, money is not as valuable as other things. You might say, "Because of your excellence in complaint-seeking performance since the last review, I'd like to raise your pay by $30 a week. Would that be all right? Or would you like to talk about a different form of recognition, such as different working conditions, a longer lunch hour, extra time off each week, or something else?" Some people might value these other things much more than the money and thus be much happier at less cost to you. You have to be courageous enough to try first.

Incentive Programs

Here, the program itself is not a motivator, but a method of distributing rewards other than those mentioned above. These are games and contests that can often strike sparks of enthusiasm and motivation in your employees. Naturally, the aim is to improve your customer service and your business. Most people respond with excitement to challenges and the chance to win recognition and tangible rewards. What you want to do is convert employees to winners, right? What better way than an incentive program that identifies plenty of winners? No longer do people have to wonder whether they should consider their latest pay raise a concession or a real reward for great performance. If the employee has just won a trip to Florida, there's no doubt he or she is a winner!

None of the foregoing tips on rewards will mean a thing if you don't understand this bit of human nature: People are motivated by many different things. It's perhaps true that everybody is motivated by money because that's the method we've customarily used to keep score in this country. Just as often, other forms of reward are much more important. If you really want to know what motivates your people, what rewards they are seeking, what ways you can use to help them achieve the status of winner, try asking them. Then and only then will the laundry list above do any good.

Follow these steps faithfully and watch the results. If you adopt the same philosophy in all your other management techniques, who knows what might happen? You might motivate somebody. You might even pump some genuine, positive sunshine into the life of *your* Old Lady Sunshine, which will automatically pump new life into your word-of-mouth marketing program.

What if that doesn't work? You may just have to get rid of her after all.

Hiring and Firing

The question is, what if you are unable to develop the superstars who will generate the most powerful, most positive word of mouth? *Your best bet is to hire superstars in the first place.*

Effective training cannot overcome the deficits of a haphazard hiring program. Lee Iacocca himself could not devise motivation techniques to reverse consistently poor hiring practices. You simply must develop a system for finding and hiring winners!

Once you find winners, everything will begin working properly. Your training program will pick up impetus and become more effective, and your management techniques will begin working better. Morale will improve. You'll be well on the way to becoming a customer service legend with a viable word-of-mouth marketing program.

Tom Peters concludes that there are only two kinds of managers, those who believe most of their people are turkeys and those who believe their people are mostly winners. And, he says, both managers are right! He says this is true because managers, in effect, create behavior that reflects their own attitudes.

The idea that managers create self-fulfilling prophecies is not at all difficult for me to believe. Every time I enter a business where the prevailing attitude is the belief that customers and employees take advantage of management, I find a management that has created exactly that problem.

In a recent telephone consultation, I spoke to William, who runs a successful business in the Southwest. With one exception, he could write a book on managing and building a profitable operation. However, his single exception, and the source of 99 percent of his problems, lies in one word, *people*. The three big mistakes William makes with people are these:

- **He has given up the belief he will ever find a superstar, and therefore, he hires too quickly.**

- **He is suspicious of new employees and immediately works to find their faults. Since everybody has faults, he's never disappointed.**

- **He turns on them and, all too soon, they're fired. Or they quit.**

Then William begins all over at step one.

William is not alone. More often than not, I find the worst cases of stinginess, mistrust, and dishonesty in the people in charge. The very managers who worry most are usually trying to get something for nothing, but they expend enormous amounts of energy trying to beat somebody out of something. They simply don't care about people, and the entire business reflects it.

If you don't believe what I've just told you, I suggest you put this book down and go guard the back door. There are probably a whole lot of turkeys stealing you blind this very minute.

If you do believe me, there's something you can do about it.

A Program for Hiring Superstars

JOB DEFINITION

You must continually define what tasks you want done in your jobs. Job descriptions must be functional and up to date. You can no more hire without a list of tasks than you can train people without knowing what behavior you want at the end of training exercises. Most important of all, they have to be specific enough to describe a job for which qualified people can be hired.

In interviewing at all kinds of companies from great to awful, I find—especially in the non-giant companies—managers are all too often guilty of hiring a person and then fitting a job to the personality, instead of defining a job and finding a person to fit it. This causes problems in nearly every case, because it's nearly impossible to determine goals if you haven't set tasks. Naturally, you can't measure effectiveness because you don't have standards. It's impossible to praise with any degree of accuracy, and any hope of training and disciplining is lost in a vague fog.

To avoid this, establish a task list. Use these guidelines for job task lists.

1. List no more than 20 tasks for a job.

2. Each task should be accompanied by a standard.

3. Each task should require no more than a 30-word sentence to describe it. The same length requirement applies to each standard.

4. The boss, the manager, and the incumbent in the job should work together to arrive at the tasks and standards.

5. Each should arrange the list according to priority from most

important to least important. (This ought to be an enlightening exercise! You'll be amazed at how often misunderstandings can be cleared up once everybody sees that different priorities have existed.) Set these tasks into priority from 1 to 20.

6. Use this valuable job description in several ways: (a) discuss the task list with every person who has that job and modify it for every position *or* demand that people in those positions modify their behavior and job performance to accomplish the tasks to the standards that have been set; (b) put the list of 20 in a tickler or suspense file so you will be reminded to review it in 90 days. Thereafter, plan to review it every six months and before hiring or promoting to fill vacancies; and chop off the bottom 14 tasks! That's right—go looking for the best candidate possible to fill the six most important tasks for that job.

JOB APPLICATION

Let's begin with some universal rules about formal, written employment applications. Use them! Use them primarily to screen out misfits and undesirables, as well as to seek information upon which to base a hiring decision. Use them for every level of job, even if you have to develop different forms for entry level employees, managers, and officers. The Universal Underwriters group says, "the important thing to remember is that relying solely on your instincts is not the wisest way to make a hiring decision. Be careful and thorough when hiring your employees. Do some checking and ask the right questions. The investment of time and money you spend at the start may save you dollars in the end."

The reason Universal Underwriters recommends being so careful is the $7 billion loss to American businesses every year due to employee theft.

Yes, I do remember telling you to be positive about people and not to mistrust everybody, but I never said you had to be blind, stupid, or obtuse about your hiring practices. You must be responsibly careful. Your people won't respect a nincompoop who leaves the store safe unlocked overnight any more than they'd respect a boss who strip-searched workers at the end of a shift.

Address specific prerequisites for a given job. Every blank job application should be accompanied by a sheet that lists mandatory and preferred (which might be waived) prerequisites and the top six tasks and standards for the job. This permits the applicant to conduct the first screening. The person who can't meet the prerequisites and won't meet the standards won't bother. Those who lie about it can be checked out.

Check out the entries in the application. Check as many as you can. Find out about time gaps. Talk to previous employers. Make a credit check with a credit bureau or credit association.

Ask for at least one reference on the formal written application, and check with the reference.

THE INTERVIEW

Once you've screened the applicants, look at a handful of the best qualified candidates in person. You should talk to no fewer than three and no more than five people.

You might begin by doing the talking first. You should describe your emphasis—your insistence—upon excellence in customer service. You should describe the company goals and objectives, plan, expected behavior, training, and rewards—all the things mentioned earlier. The purpose of this discussion is to lay out the path to success in your company and to highlight customer service.

Then you get down to the specifics of the job, the tasks you've defined, and the standards you will demand in the top six tasks. Here is the time to look for the strengths needed to accomplish what you want done. Once you're satisfied a candidate possesses the strengths to accomplish your top six, you can look past the top six tasks for a candidate's additional strengths. The strongest candidates will be able to accomplish the most tasks and thus require less training.

Along the way, you will find weaknesses—they will crop up. These limitations must be examined in any enlightened hiring decision, but your litmus test always goes back to the top six and is framed by the question: "Can this person do the major aspects of the job?" When you get to weaknesses further down the line of tasks, you have to ask if this limitation will be so severe as to diminish the capacity to get the desired job done. Don't let personal weaknesses not related to performance on

the central job—or personal strengths not related, for that matter—
become too strong an influence on your decision.

During this entire process, you will be measuring the candidate
against those standards you expect to see in the superstars you want to
hire.

THE FINAL QUESTION BEFORE HIRING

"Could I fire this person?" should be the final question you ask yourself.
Never hire somebody you can't fire!

Is it the son of your best customer? Is it a best friend or a relative? No
matter how well you perform recruiting and interviewing, it's possible
to be tricked. In those cases, you simply have to cut your losses and fire
the turkey who slipped through all your screens and turned out not to
be a superstar after all. But you must ask yourself that question *before*
you offer the job. You must ask, "Could I fire this person?" If the answer
is "Yes," do one more thing. Call or visit the references the applicant has
given. If the references check out, go ahead. Hire that person.

The Firing Phase

I didn't refer to this as a phase before, but it is. That's because the last
item you discuss with a new employee about the road to success is the
procedure for firing. Every employee has the right to know when they're
going down the road to termination.

I know what I'm talking about. You see, I was fired once. The really
bad part about the firing was that I never had a clue it was coming. I
didn't know I was doing anything wrong until I was told to leave for not
meeting standards I had never heard of until I got fired! It's left me very
sensitive to the issue of firing.

Like it or not, firing happens to be part of the management process.
When it happens in the way it happened to me, it can be as devastating
for an employee as a divorce or the death of a loved one. Imagine the
shock, depression, anger, guilt, embarrassment, and confusion that can
result when a firing comes, especially when it comes without warning.

Never be guilty of this. When you hire using my system, you've already given warning about the path to firing. Let me show you how to fire someone and have them thank you.

THE FIRST WARNING

When you find misconduct or unsatisfactory performance in the areas of your non-negotiable rules, you'll have to act with a warning. Otherwise, they're no longer non-negotiables. Repeated misbehavior in lesser offenses can become just as serious as major offenses. Don't collect these offenses until you're angry enough to fly off the handle. Deal with them as they occur and you'll find the emotional level remains low. Give specific oral warnings. Use the five R's of an oral first warning:

1. **Refer** to the rule that was broken. Be specific, and be serious.

2. **Recite** the behavior that you identified as being in violation.

3. **Recess,** so the employee can tell his or her side of the story. You will want to identify a mistaken report of misbehavior.

4. **Reprimand** the behavior; don't attack the person.

5. **Review** the consequences of repeated misconduct. If repeats will lead to firing, say so.

After you've reprimanded, don't refer back to this incident casually. You don't have to forget it, but you certainly don't want to broadcast that you're carrying a grudge. Let an employee prove the misbehavior will not happen again.

THE SECOND WARNING

Now's the time to show things have gotten serious. You might refer back to the oral briefing upon repeats of misconduct or poor performance. Go ahead and use the five R's again, but this time put the rule, the misbehavior, and the consequences in writing. Use a probationary period if you want, but you'd be just as well off telling an employee at this point that he or she is on permanent probation. Writing down bad things is the first step on the road to termination. The oral correction of a mistake won't be seen as a step toward firing. Even a stern oral first warning doesn't have to be seen as a move toward termination. But the moment you commit something to writing, you've begun.

You must make certain that your employee knows the next incident will lead to that firing, but you must be just as determined your employee knows you are more interested in success. Tell the person you want to salvage this horrible situation. Repeat your positive commitment to finding strengths in people. You must repeat all over again—just as with new employees—the path to success.

If you do this, you'll be asking whether the person really wants to go down that road to success or to take the just as clearly defined road to termination. These persons will make their own decisions. They will straighten themselves out . . . *or they will fire themselves*! They will even thank you for giving them the opportunity to succeed and for showing them they could be better off in a different career field.

The Last Word on Hiring and Firing

It's your responsibility. If you have a company full of turkeys, it's your fault. If your hiring practices reek, blame yourself. You don't have to wear sackcloth and ashes, but you must face the problems in this most important area head-on. You see, it isn't the turkey's fault that he's a turkey, but it's your fault for hiring him or keeping him on. On the other hand, the superstars are your responsibility, too. You can find and hire winners.

SUMMARY OF CHAPTER 10

◆ Rule Ten: Catch your employees generating positive word of mouth and reward them for it.

◆ Compliment wisely. Praise behavior you want to reinforce. Be sincere, specific, immediate, public, and personal. Never qualify your praise by adding a negative shade to it.

◆ Learn to use the tangible and intangible motivators: the performance appraisal, time, the promotion, the pay raise, and other incentives.

◆ Hire winners and fire losers. Define the job using a task list. Hire for the six most important tasks you want your employee to fulfill.

◆ Never hire somebody you can't fire.

◆ Take responsibility for firing. Fire as painlessly as possible. Give effective warnings. Follow these prefiring steps on the first warning:

- Refer to the broken rule.

- Recite the improper behavior.

- Recess so the employee can put in a word.

- Reprimand behavior, not people.

- Review the consequences of continued improper behavior.

11

Boss Behavior That Converts Word-of-Mouth Marketing Strategies into Action!

The final chapter in this section is about leadership. What's the difference between management and leadership? Books have been written about the differences. To me, it can be stated very simply: Managers get things together—leaders get things done!

Somebody said, "There are three kinds of people: those who make things happen, those who watch things happen, and those who wonder what happened." Leaders make things happen.

Getting things done through leadership is the point of this chapter.

Rule Eleven: For a word-of-mouth marketing plan to work, an organization's leaders must commit to active, proven practices for getting things done.

What Gets Talked About Gets Done

Boss talk begets manager talk begets employee talk begets . . . Did you ever read about "mirroring" in an article or book on body language? According to those who study such things, one person in conversation often subconsciously tries to win favor or show understanding by subconsciously mirroring the posture of the other person. If the speaker is clasping both hands over one knee or crossing one ankle over another, the listener does the same thing. Pay attention sometime when employees speak with a boss. The boss nods—so does the employee. The boss leans forward—so does the employee. The same things happen in verbal language. I've been to management meetings where the boss introduces a new expression in the morning and by afternoon every conversation in the secretarial pool is sprinkled with the same term.

Don't try to analyze people's motives for doing so, but when the boss shows he or she is interested by continually talking about things such as stopping the horror talk, installing no hassle, seeking complaints, delivering legendary customer service, and exceeding expectations, everybody in the company listens. When that boss talk is emphatically repeated and finally appears in written form, even the dullest employees get the idea. When subordinate managers and leaders begin echoing the boss's words, the principles are reinforced. The line and staff pick up on general themes and specific programs, and an organization becomes universally aware of what the boss stands for. If that talk can become infected with enthusiasm, so much the better. People will not only adhere to the formal spoken and written rules of behavior associated with boss talk, they will develop an informal code of behavior that is in keeping with the spirit of the boss's philosophy.

There are a couple of cautions that you might know already or could deduce on your own after a few bad experiences. Say what you mean. Draft the exact word of mouth message you want to convey. Try it out on your best advisers, your spouse, a focus group of customers, and a focus group of employees. That way you won't find yourself backtracking because you seem confused and unprepared. Then say it with conviction. Tell everybody that you've committed to a solid word-of-mouth marketing program. Let everybody know you have the staying power to make it work.

Mean what you say. Talk alone isn't enough. Making a one-time speech won't cut it. You must be consistent, continuous, and creative in sending the message you want adopted throughout your business or organization. This is the message you want transmitted to your base of customers or public. That's what reputations—images—are. You will have to back up your words with actions. Your first action is to set the example. Here are some tips for leaders on being a role model.

General Behavior and Demeanor

In this respect, bosses are role models exactly like parents to their employees. Remember instances of "do as I say, not as I do" in your childhood, such as when your father or mother told you to finish all the food on your plate and then left something on his or her own plate? No matter how much you loved your parents, you couldn't help noticing the irony—even the hypocrisy—in those events. Now, generally speaking, parents have in their favor love and forgiveness from their children. An employer doesn't have that kind of head start. Your employees are continually watching your behavior, your dress, your habits, and the other clues to your character. They are looking both for faults to criticize and for things to emulate. You must set the example you want to see in your people.

Behave toward customers exactly as you wish your employees to behave toward them. Dress for customer service as you wish to see the other front line troops dress when they deal with customers. Most importantly, treat your people as you wish them to treat customers. If you release your aggressions on your employees, don't be surprised if you see the resentment passed along to customers.

If you want a company rule followed, follow it yourself. If you want your people to eat in your own cafeteria, it's imperative you be seen eating there yourself. Your employees will come in early and stay late to complete an emergency project, usually because you attach some reward to the extra work, but if you also share in the extra hours, they will be motivated far beyond the value of any tangibles you put in their bonus stocking.

Demonstrate the Appropriate Level of Expertness.

Especially in matters of customer service, you should be able to perform all the tasks you expect of your employees in customer service. You should know all your own policies and follow them. Usually it's impossible to be a role model of excellence in customer service if you do not possess some capability for excellence yourself. When you become defensive with an angry customer, fan the customer's emotions, verbally abuse the customer, eject the customer from the store, or then denigrate the customer thoroughly (I have witnessed all of this behavior by a store manager in the presence of his employees), don't be surprised when you witness that in your employees. On the other hand, if you're so smooth and considerate, the customer's emotions are soothed, and you win a big order, all your people will learn from your expert example. They will set you up as their role model. When that kind of situation occurs, you have begun to achieve legendary customer service.

Thoroughly Understand Standards of Excellence Beyond Your Own Ability to Demonstrate

Let me borrow from one of the U.S. Army's best writers and most insightful observers of leaders, General S. L. A. Marshall. He wrote his remarks, which I'll paraphrase, in a Department of Defense manual. Usually you don't have to know more about computer programming than your programmers. You don't ordinarily have to demonstrate greater knowledge of electronics repair than your technicians. You don't have to prove you can mop a floor or install plumbing better than your maintenance and engineering experts in order to set a good example. If you set that kind of unreasonable standard for yourself, you'd soon be considered a member of the lunatic fringe. Setting the example in this age of specialization does not require you to be able to do everything that your specialists do for you. That is unreasonable to expect of yourself, and your employees don't expect it either.

However, you should know the difference between the power to do a thing well and the ability to judge when it is well done. A woman can determine that a book is well written without being a writer herself, if she is a student of the literature she's judging. A man doesn't have to lay an egg to know a good omelette when he tastes one. All he needs is a little knowledge of cooking and a fair sampling of many good eggs and a few bad ones.

When You Can't Be the Role Model, Establish Who the Role Models Ought To Be

When you're a winning baseball coach who couldn't hit the side of a barn with the ball, you don't give up teaching that aspect of the game, do you? No, you set up your best hitter as the role model, or you even might point out the best attributes of your opposition's best hitter. You might even set up a professional baseball player as the role model and show films of him to teach hitting.

Be Wary of Unhealthy Competition

It shouldn't matter to your ego if your employees become better than you, their role model. If they've become winners whose performance exceeds your own, that's exactly what you're seeking. Don't fall prey to the temptation to best your people at everything. Be the best role model you can. When your standards are bested by somebody else's performance or behavior, do the smart thing: Make that person the new role model!

What Gets Trained for Gets Done

You must train your people in the principles of word-of-mouth marketing. Training is not a management function. Training is a leadership function. You need training managers, and your managers should oversee and conduct training, but *training is a function of leadership.* The central segment of a word-of-mouth marketing program is great service, and you must train people for it. If a training program of any kind is to succeed, the boss must get behind it. Only then will you get action.

How many times have you been waited on by a fumbling clerk who messed up your order, totaled your receipt wrong, and failed to return your credit card? Just before you explode, the person usually says, "Sorry, this is my first day on the job."

If you're like me, you bite back your anger and try to be more patient with the new person. On the other hand, you probably wonder what this company's leaders have on their minds in letting the customer suffer through the bad experience of a new employee.

You really can't afford to let every new employee learn the customer service ropes through experience. That's because too many of those experiences are apt to be bad ones. It's not smart to let inexperienced employees start ugly stories about your service.

Contrast that with your experiences at the companies legendary for customer service. It seems they *never* have new employees. In truth, they do, but the new people are so well trained from the very beginning, you can't tell they're new!

Training is essential because of the three ways customers judge your business:

- That critical first impression your people make on the customer.

- Your employees' ability to solve their problems, that is, to fulfill the customer's needs and wants.

- The distinctiveness of your employees' ability to deliver customer service, that is, whether it's awful or legendary.

In other words, your customers are going to judge your business by three things: your employees, your employees, and your employees. How can you afford *not* to train them to meet the challenge?

In my opinion, next to a failure to plan, the biggest deficiency in most businesses today is a lack of training programs. Even successful businesses could profit by more attention to training. In my experience as a consultant, I often see payroll and benefits consuming 20 to 50 percent of the gross revenues of small businesses. Yet little or nothing is budgeted for training. Every week paychecks are written for thousands of dollars and not a dime is spent to give deserving employees the tools they need to do their jobs better.

There are three reasons why companies *should* train. First, the benefits include professionalism, consistency in the quality of products and services, efficiency, employee pride, and so on. Second, training is an investment in the longevity of a company. You know the captain of an aircraft carrier can't possibly stay on duty every hour of the day. Sooner or later, he must turn over command of the bridge to another well-trained, responsible officer and go below decks. Surely you suspect he would never pick the first sailor who happened by and say, "Here are the keys to the boat. Take her for a spin around the harbor." No, the captain turns command over to a well-trained officer.

IBM employees spend an average of 15 days a year in formal training. As you know, IBM is on everybody's list for excellence. Shouldn't you take a hint from that company and garner your own corner in the excellence marketplace?

Third, setting up a training program is simply not difficult.

The Skeleton of Every Training Program

There may be thousands of businesses needing thousands of training programs and every one might have a different training need from every other business. We're only talking here about the essence of customer service training, but you're going to be surprised at how many of the descriptions, principles, and accounts of customer service training apply universally to every training situation imaginable.

The first of these universals is the framework of training, the skeleton. Begin by asking three questions:

1. What result do we want?
2. What standards must be met to achieve the desired result?
3. What training will ensure the standards are met?

Now let's answer each question.

WHAT RESULT DO WE WANT IN CUSTOMER SERVICE TRAINING?

We want our customers to feel as if they receive the greatest service imaginable. Define this in the form of a mission or goal. Then quantify it in the form of objectives. Form an overall plan. Now the process requires no more than translating our objectives into human terms. For starters, we need a training goal. How about this: Our customer service training aims to improve the knowledge, behavior, or attitudes of our employees so our customers believe they're getting the greatest service possible!

That wasn't too difficult. Now let's go on to the second question.

WHAT STANDARDS MUST BE MET TO ACHIEVE THE DESIRED RESULT?

Your guides for setting training standards in customer service are affected by the nature of the competition and marketplace—the customer service position you want to stake out for yourself; the customer's needs, wants, and problems; and your desire to excel—in the words of James Hawkins, to become legendary in customer service.

Start setting standards with the eight ways customers judge your employees:

1. Appearance
2. Method of greeting
3. Facial expressions
4. Body language
5. Knowledge of the product or service
6. What they say and how they say it
7. How well they listen
8. Sincerity and enthusiasm

The training standards for each of these areas takes too much space to address every one. Let's use the method of greeting as an example.

■ **Minimal standards.** You might not ever have thought about this, it's so obvious. I can't tell you how many times I walk into a place of business and am immediately put off by the greeting I receive. The all-time worst for me is, "Hey, Bud, can I hep ya?"

This is an area where it's easy to set non-negotiable standards— "my way or the highway." It's easy to check. It's easy to maintain a standard if you inspect what you expect. Whereas you might have trouble enforcing a hair grooming standard, you have every right to demand your employees use precise words and actions in greeting a customer.

Some minimum standards I always insist upon:

- First and foremost, the customer must be greeted, not ignored. How many times have you approached a cash register wearing your "invisible clothing" so the clerk filling the cigarette stacks couldn't see you and serve you?
- The employee must use "ma'am" or "sir" in addressing the customer. If the customer's name is known, then it's "Mr.," "Mrs.," "Miss," or "Ms."

■ **Standards of excellence.** To achieve excellence, you'll have to really work. If many of the touches in appearance are self-evident, the approach to a customer will require some work to master.

- The customer must be greeted within 15 seconds of entering your place of business.
- The employee must always look into the customer's eyes while greeting him or her.
- The employee must give his or her name in greeting the customer and also must ask for and use the customer's name immediately upon learning it.
- The employee must immediately and actively listen to find the customer's needs, wants, and problems.

WHAT TRAINING WILL ENSURE THAT THE STANDARDS ARE MET?

When setting up training, use the **IDEAL** method of training

IDEAL is an acronym that stands for the following steps:

Identify the standard.
Demonstrate the standard.
Employee demonstrates mastery of the standard.
Adjust performance to correct continued shortfalls.
Lavish praise when the standard is met or exceeded.

Identify the standard

Give your standards in writing and draw a picture where the key points are highlighted. State your standard in positive terms. For example, "This training is going to help each of us be judged excellent by our customers. That will improve the company's profits and give every one of us a better chance for advancement."

Demonstrate the standard

It is a fundamental rule of leadership that you should *never* chastise somebody for unsatisfactory behavior or performance when you've never showed the person what the standards for satisfactory performance were. Demonstrate the task properly and take questions in this step.

Employee demonstrates mastery of the standard

Once the training standard is demonstrated, your people should be given the chance to practice it without fear of penalty. There are a couple of proven guidelines to use in this part of the exercise.

- Ask every employee trained to demonstrate mastery of the training standard.

- Require this demonstration as soon as possible after the training by the instructor. This prevents the loss of learning that is caused by forgetfulness.

- Allow room for failure without embarrassment. Let employees practice in low-risk situations or in privacy.

- Begin keeping records of training. Two reasons to do this are reward and punishment. You will want to repay great performance, and you will want to avoid hearing excuses such as, "Nobody ever told me."

Adjust performance to correct continued shortfalls

Give helpful hints—tips and tricks of the trade—to encourage success. Point out the pitfalls and traps in the performance.

Lavish praise when the standard is exceeded. Use positive reinforcement. You almost never have to tell a youngster in the Little League outfield that he made a mistake when the ball bounced off his nose. The kid knows it. Perhaps it's intuition. Or maybe it's just the pain on the nose and a trickle of blood. Trust me, a kid who drops a fly ball *knows* he's made a mistake. Yet there are parents and coaches who will scream at children who make physical errors in sports, as in, "Bobby, you're supposed to *catch* the ball, not *drop* it."

Well, that is just nonproductive nonsense. Point out to a child that when running after a fly ball, it's best to run up on the balls of the feet instead of the heels because the ball won't dance in the vision as much— that's coaching. Tell the child to shake off the mistake and continue playing hard—that's encouragement. Find something good about other related behavior, as in, "Way to hustle, Bobby. Nice throw."

If you look for good behavior, attitudes, and knowledge in your people, you will find them. If you begin finding a few good things and praising them, it won't be long before you begin to find even more things worthy of praise.

The lavish use of praise in training (and leadership, for that matter) is a self-fulfilling prophecy in action. Do you doubt it? The next time you're in the library or a bookstore, take a peek inside any dog training book. See what you find about the necessity of praise in animal training. If you'd praise a dog . . . .

Finally, I'll close this segment with a bonus, some training principles:

1. **Avoid abstractions and generalities.** Keep your examples specific and realistic. Use examples from your own industry— better yet, use examples from your own business or staff.

2. **Involve all the senses.** Telling requires only the involvement of the ears. Showing includes the eyes. Use as much participation

as possible in training. Some training researchers have indicated that we retain about a quarter of what we hear, half of what we see and hear, and three quarters of what we see, hear, and do.

3. **Use activities.** Right in line with involving the senses is the use of competition, games, skits and training situations that require practice and movement and especially the use of the employee's judgment.

4. **Err on the side of haste.** Don't put people to sleep by targeting your training to the lowest possible denominator of intelligence in your class. Instead, push your students to learn as fast as they can. Challenge people. This doesn't mean you leave the methodical learners in the dust or that you solicit sloppy work. You can always devote some individual attention to those who need to catch up.

5. **Train to meet your needs!!** Two exclamation points. It should be obvious, but too often, training is done for training's sake alone. You make it incredibly boring when you train a class full of students about matters in which they are already quite proficient. The primary point here is to identify shortfalls where performance, behavior, knowledge, or attitudes do not meet your standards; then train to correct the deficiencies!

    Serve it up banquet-style. You must have a complete, integrated program with a beginning, a middle, and an end, just as a fine dinner would be served. But try to avoid cramming all your training down the gullets of your people at once. You should set priorities for the most important subjects and spread out training over time to meet those priorities.

What Gets Measured Gets Done

Inspect what you expect. Someone once said, "If you don't stand for something, you're liable to fall for anything."

Domino's Pizza stands for the 30-minute delivery of hot and delicious pizza—guaranteed. Federal Express stands for overnight deliveries by

10:30 a.m. the next day—absolutely positively. A large body shop client of mine stands for cars repaired "better than new" and delivered by 5 p.m. on the day promised. A quick-lube chain brags that your car will be completely serviced in 10 minutes—or your service is half price.

Your business or organization might stand for the lowest number of quality control complaints in the industry. As a lobbyist, you might stand for the highest number of bills favorable to your cause passed in a legislative session—or the lowest number of unfavorable bills.

The point is, if you stand for something, merely by defining it, you will begin setting specific, measurable goals and objectives. On the other hand, if you find you run your operation without reference to objectives of any kind, you might just discover a horrible truth—you don't stand for anything!

Stop right here for a second and write down all the things that are important for you to measure. You can measure the time it takes for your people to meet and greet prospects, customers, and clients. Fifteen seconds from the time a person enters your place of business is a reasonable standard to set. You can measure the time it takes for somebody to answer a telephone. Three might be a standard for the maximum number of rings allowed.

You can measure the number of mail orders in a working day. You can measure the length of your Sunday sermons. You can measure line time in your fast food restaurant—the time customers wait from your front door to the food counter. You can measure the number of videocassette recorders (VCRs) repaired in a day, you can determine the length of time a VCR waits before being ready for return, and you can measure the percentage of VCRs that come back because they were not fixed correctly the first time.

I can't tell you the entire range of possibilities for measurement you can have in your field, but I can tell you that measurements are critical. Next, setting a standard of performance is essential. It is a factor that goes hand in hand with training. Here are a few tips for measuring in your business, company, or organization:

■ Make sure everyone in your operation is aware of what measurable goals and standard you have set. Let people know these will be inspected, day in and day out. Make certain they understand this inspection isn't a check to catch people—it's a method of measuring the continual legendary delivery of your goods and services. Let people know you can be understanding of occasional system failures and disruptions outside their control, but when you *inspect* your standards you *expect* those standards will be met.

■   Teach everyone what's important. They will in turn set up their own measurement criteria. Everyone from the CEO to part-time custodial workers must know what you stand for and what you *won't* stand for.

■   Set up a system to measure your results regularly. Some results must be measured hourly, some daily, and others monthly. Some transactions can be measured against your standard by selecting a representative sample and extrapolating results. Others—as in the case of the Oklahoma restaurant that put a timer on every table and promised lunch in 15 minutes—can be measured with every single transaction.

■   Measure the critical few and avoid the many. In the years Robert McNamara served as Secretary of Defense, the Pentagon went through a period of trying to measure everything. An entire industry within the defense industry grew up around the bureaucracy of measurement. In Vietnam, it was this system that gave us the discredited "body count" method of measuring battlefield success. Since everything was measured, everything was important, with the most important thing at the moment being the things measured at the moment. Decide what is critical to the success of a word-of-mouth marketing program. Measure that and let the other things take care of themselves.

■   Involve everybody. American business is still learning an expensive lesson from the Japanese. Shove responsibility for measurement down the line to the person performing the task. Give everybody standards to achieve, train them to perform, and put them in charge of inspecting themselves.

■   Don't settle for excuses. Define the non-negotiable standards among the critical few areas of measurement. As a leader, you might accept valid explanations for failure to meet standards, but you cannot ignore your standards once set and inspected. If you allow continual excuses, you are sending a message that the standard isn't important. Do something. Revise the standard. Improve the methods for attaining the standard. Add more resources for getting the standard met. Replace those who can't perform to standards. If the standard is really important enough for you to take action to see it gets met, your people will take you seriously. Do you want to know the absolutely best way to design a system that does not accept excuses? Instead of demanding people respond to you or to a cumbersome set of standards, make them responsible to themselves. Set up a system that pays incentives when subordinate leaders succeed—and that does not pay when they fail. They will feel that they have an investment in your organization because they have some control, and your standards will be met.

- When it's broke, fix it *fast*. This is just another way for your people to get the message that you want emphasis on a standard that you and they are measuring. They will very quickly learn to report deviations from standard and either fix it themselves or get assistance.

- You can't afford to limit your measurements to internally devised standards. Invite your customers, clients, and champions to help you measure your standards. Make it easy for them to let you know of their experiences when they inspected you and found you wanting. While researching *A Passion For Excellence*, Tom Peters and Nancy Austin found 232 company presidents who said that long-term customer satisfaction was their number one priority. Then, when asked how many measured any of their people on an impartial scale of long-term total customer satisfaction, not one president could say he or she used such a measurement. Clearly, this is an area where talk exceeds action.

- Praise those who succeed consistently in meeting and exceeding standards. What gets praised gets repeated.

- Build redundancy into the system. If you process hundreds of transactions a day that lead to customer service, which determines whether your word of mouth will be positive or negative, you can't afford to let one person bear the sole responsibility of being error-free. Have your people check each other. Remember, instill in them that the idea is not to find fault, but to make corrections before the customer has to call errors to your attention.

■ Measure the right things. Don't just collect statistics *you* think are important. Ask your customers what *they* think is important. Jan Carlzon, in *Moments of Truth*, tells how the airline he took over had always measured its performance in cargo handling by the amount of freight carried. He determined that that was a company need. Customers didn't care if he filled the bellies of his aircraft. They were concerned about prompt delivery to the correct location. He set a goal: "To become the airline with the highest precision." His cargo people reported that only a small percentage of shipments went awry. Then he tested his system, sending 100 packages to various addresses.

"The results were devastating," he says. "The small parcels were supposed to arrive the next day; however, the average was four days later. Our precision was terrible.

"We had caught ourselves in one of the most basic mistakes a service-oriented business can make: promising one thing and measuring another." His cargo people had been measuring only whether the packages and the accompanying paperwork were separated en route.

Are you measuring the right things?

■ Share your results—even when it's bad news. By letting your people know when you're hitting the mark and when you're falling short, you continually remind them that you're inspecting.

What Gets Budgeted Gets Done

If word-of-mouth marketing isn't in the budget, it isn't. Establish word-of-mouth marketing as a budget item and never look back. Set aside funds as an investment that pays you dividends. Every year, conduct the same kind of budget analysis for word-of-mouth marketing that you do for payroll and other items. If you fail to put it into the budget, your commitment is suspect—word-of-mouth marketing will fail because nobody (including you, apparently) sees it as a serious undertaking.

What Gets Applauded Gets Done

Praise pays. I think I discussed this amply in Chapter 10, don't you? Remember, praise is just another form of word of mouth that can be made systematic, intentional, and productive.

What Gets Rewarded Gets Done

Praise pays but it doesn't pay the mortgage. Face it, sometimes you must use more tangible incentives in connection with praise to get that extra mile out of your people in putting an effective word-of-mouth marketing program into action. Besides those motivators discussed in the previous chapter, here's another incentive a leader might use: involvement.

Get your people committed to your company to the extent they really believe it's theirs. They'd like to do this anyhow—it's a natural inclination to want to own things. Usually people take care of things they own better than they care for things that belong to some nebulous *them*.

Strategies for Getting Employees Involved

■ **Share the planning and goal setting.** Does it sound fruitless to ask a dock worker for input about how to lower customer complaints? Who knows better about damage, delays in transportation, packaging, and handling than the men and women who have to lug your products around? Ask your people in every facet of the business about improving customer service planning. Invite employees to staff meetings. Walk around the business and ask them their feelings about the meetings they attended, the practicality of the goals that have been set, the plans that have been made. If you can be sincere—and can take a bit of criticism or needling without any form of actual or perceived retaliation—you'll soon find a wealth of new ideas.

- **Give your employees responsibility and authority—then get out of their hair and let them do their jobs.** Nothing is more demeaning than to have to run to the boss every time a decision is required. Sharing your responsibilities gives people a stake in getting things done, things you can't always do personally. Sharing authority—giving responsible people the power to make their own decisions in their areas of accountability—is the second most important thing in sharing. Let your people make on-the-spot decisions and solve problems.

- **Give them room to make mistakes.** Nobody's perfect. Along with responsibility, authority, and accountability to the boss must go the understanding that misbehavior, immorality, and malfeasance won't be tolerated, but honest mistakes won't be fatal. Yes, it's taking a risk, but you must trust others to grow personally and professionally. Not even Alexander the Great could personally lead every unit of his conquering armies. Many are the generals and corporate leaders who have learned that lesson the hard way.

  There are two areas where you don't want mistakes. One is in areas of employee safety; the other is in customer service. Don't let inexperienced people make their mistakes on customers—remember that mistakes that enrage your customers will result in horror stories, that negative word of mouth.

- **Implement the unique ideas—*and give credit where it is due!*** Anybody of reasonable intelligence and with knowledge of the business ought to be able to recognize a good idea. Seeking great ideas is another matter. Use what works best for you—meetings, brainstorming sessions, quality circles, contests, and just walking around talking are all workable ways. Believe me, every great idea you use will net you two or three more if you follow this advice:

- Use the ideas suggested
- Take action immediately
- Publicize the source of the idea
- Don't let intermediate managers "steal" ideas from subordinates
- Reward the suggester

What Gets Reprimanded Gets Done

Sometimes you just have to chew somebody out! Let's face it, being blunt and harsh has its place.

A reprimand is merely another form of talk that's sometimes the most effective of all. I don't want to contradict Chapter 10, where I stated that people are only motivated by positives, such as the expectation of reward, but I suppose I'll have to. Yes, some people do need to be motivated by fear once in a while. You sometimes have to express it in the form of a reprimand.

If some people in your organization can't seem to join in the word-of-mouth marketing program, leaders have to make the corrections. It's obvious. If you permit word-of-mouth marketing to fall by the wayside in a few cases today, you're likely to have a few more cases tomorrow. Here are a few tips on the chewing-out:

- ■ **Keep your cool.** Don't blow up and instigate an argument. After all, we've been discussing a pervasive attitude throughout a company, an attitude that is cultivated so thoroughly that it characterizes every contact with customers and clients outside the company too.

- ■ **State the problem to the employee in a friendly way.** Who knows? Maybe this person doesn't even know he or she is upsetting you or the word-of-mouth marketing apple cart.

- ■ **Get the employee to evaluate the situation with you.** Maybe the person can tell you causes you hadn't thought of.

- ■ **Ask the person to suggest ways of fixing things.** It's very likely an employee knows the solution. Try to get employee involvement in the solution to help in finding ways he or she might improve.

- **Cooperate, or at least agree to a solution,** including a specific time by which the problem will be corrected.

- **Follow up.** On the appointed date, review the situation. Make additional corrections. Praise or reward, if appropriate.

SUMMARY OF CHAPTER 11

- ◆ Rule Eleven: For a word-of-mouth marketing plan to work, an organization's leaders must commit to active, proven practices for getting things done.

- ◆ What gets talked about gets done. Leaders must be role models who say what they mean and mean what they say.

- ◆ What gets trained for gets done. You must train your people in the principles of word-of-mouth marketing. Training is a leadership function, built on a framework of answering the following three questions:
  - What result do we want in customer service training?
  - What standards must be met to achieve the desired result?
  - What training will ensure that the standards are met?

- ◆ What gets measured gets done.

- ◆ What gets budgeted gets done.

- ◆ What gets applauded gets done.

- ◆ What gets rewarded gets done

- ◆ What gets reprimanded gets done.

The Word-of-Mouth Marketing Blitz

> "This is *not* rocket science."
>
> **—Anonymous**

12

The Word-of-Mouth Marketing Blitz: An Exercise in Simplicity

As it turns out, I first used a word-of-mouth marketing blitz before I even knew what it was. In 1980, I took over a state trade association, a business on the brink of disaster. I muddled my way through a turnaround of that association using techniques I have finally given names in the writing of this book. Between that first blitz and the completion of this book, I've added quite a bit to my knowledge of the word-of-mouth marketing blitz. In fact, I've tried the proven techniques and developed a few new ones in the marketing of this book. In Chapter 13 you will read the case study of the word-of-mouth marketing blitz I used in marketing *Word-of-Mouth Marketing*, this book. I suggest you skim this chapter, and the next to see how certain techniques mentioned here were applied in real blitzes. Then read both chapters to see how the practice compares to the technique.

In this section of the book, we first must tie all the loose ends together. Ideally, you will have mastered the dynamics of word-of-mouth marketing, as described in Section I. Then, your organization would have engaged in the practices of Section II to establish, build, and maintain a consistent, enduring company reputation with everybody who talks about you. Finally, on any occasion that demanded, you could put a word-of-mouth marketing blitz team together to launch a new product or service, to reverse the effects of a company public relations disaster, or to build a new image. Because of your mastery of the earlier material, a blitz would come to you and your people as automatically as breathing.

The starting place is that first rule of word-of-mouth marketing. No matter how much you spend on advertising, no matter how clever your slogans, no matter how aggressive your sales force, you can't make it in business without a good product or service. By now, it should be obvious to you that it would be a mistake to use any form of the *talk factor* to launch a word-of-mouth marketing campaign for an inferior product or service. By definition, the campaign would spread bad news even farther.

If you've followed that first rule and can keep the others in mind, you are ready to launch your new product or service.

Rule Twelve: Keep your word-of-mouth marketing campaign plan simple but systematic—in short, *streamline everything and orient everything to action!*

Your first step was to identify the product or service worthy of a word-of-mouth marketing blitz. Next, identify the mission, put together a creative team, give the team some tools to do the job, and get out of the way. Let's look at some of these elements for success.

The Word-of-Mouth Marketing Blitz Team

Identify the Mission

For you, the leader, this means no more than to state what you want done. Maybe you want to introduce a new logo to the marketplace in a way that continually reassures existing and potential customers and clients that your company is healthy and growing with the times. That's a mission.

Maybe you'd like to counter the effect of a product recall with a series of new initiatives to restore customer confidence. That's a mission.

Perhaps you'd like to see this year's annual clearance sale reverse a trend of declining profits you've seen in the past three sales. Again, a mission.

When I took over as executive director of my state trade association, the Indiana Automotive Wholesalers Association, I found that the mission was merely to exist. Since the organization was shrinking every year in membership and running in the red, I declared an emergency to save it. I ran from one end of the state to the other, determined to keep the IAWA in existence. It was the wrong thing to do. That was not a practical mission at all. After I'd exhausted myself with furious activity and little result, I collected the people I trusted and sat down to examine every single aspect of our association. Nothing was sacred. The first thing to be challenged was the mission. Simply to exist wasn't enough. So I wrote a new mission: to give our members the products and services to help them become more profitable and professional. We all realized that succeeding in such a mission would not only ensure our existence— it would make us prosper.

When I began my own word-of-mouth marketing blitz for this book, my mission was simply to make it a best seller. My vision included any number of details that translated into objectives in my word-of-mouth marketing action plan.

What is *your* vision? By sharing a clear concept of your vision with the word-of-mouth marketing blitz team, you establish a common long range goal for the team members. Turn that vision into a simple mission statement. The emphasis is on *simple*. In my opinion, you shouldn't even bother trying to express your mission statement in the form of a breakdown of objectives with measurables like time, money, customers, percentages, and so on. Leave that to the blitz team.

Have you got it? Now you're ready to put together that creative team.

Organizing a Word-of-Mouth Marketing Blitz Team

Pick the brightest minds with the most willing backs and throw them together. Don't worry too much about organizational charts and titles that exist in the day-to-day operation of your business. You're working on something extraordinary. You want results that are anything but ordinary business-as-usual. Pick a handful of creative people and stand back to watch the chemistry. Don't be afraid to turn to mavericks, and don't overlook unexpected places in your search for talent. In your warehouse may be a creative, energetic employee who could add insights the white collar men and women of the marketing department wouldn't think of. Creativity alone isn't enough—look for creativity combined with a reputation for putting ideas into action.

In his book, *In Search of Excellence*, Tom Peters describes a phenomenon that embodies the entrepreneurial spirit, the so-called "skunk works." Peters writes that many companies were proud of their skunk works, "bands of eight or ten zealots off in the corner, often outproducing product development groups that numbered in the hundreds.

"It eventually became clear that all of these companies were making a purposeful trade-off. They were creating almost radical decentralization and autonomy, with its attendant overlap, messiness around the edges, lack of coordination, internal competition, and somewhat chaotic conditions, in order to breed the entrepreneurial spirit. They had forsworn a measure of tidiness in order to achieve regular innovation."

This is precisely what you want to achieve with your word-of-mouth marketing blitz team.

■   Detach blitz team activities from the normal marketing plan during the initial planning stages—don't worry about standard staff coordination at this point. If you want fresh ideas, you'll have to take a few risks here. Remember, you can keep control by managing the outcome of blitz team activities. You don't have to micro-manage every step along the way. Relieve people from routine duties for a specified period while they are members of the blitz team. If that leads to a temporary perception of elitism, so what? Give the team members a few moments in the spotlight to see what sort of brilliance can be generated. If the blitz team causes momentary turmoil, you'll survive. In my opinion, high intensity moments of turbulence often create the most dramatic results. Don't mind a few sparks—maybe the sparks will light a few fires under people who've grown stale with the humdrum of business as usual.

Perhaps you don't agree? Fine, but I've observed that three things pull a team—a blitz team, in this case—together:

- Common goals
- Common successes
- Common adversaries

You've given the team its goal—your vision in the form of a mission statement. Possibly you've set the team up and given them temporary adversaries, with the standard line of command and organizational charts. That will bind them together. Next, you will look for the common successes.

- ■ If you must give the blitz team supplemental instructions, make them mission-oriented instructions. Mission orders keep things simple. Tell your team you want an action plan that stirs up positive word of mouth. Ask for a list of no more than ten objectives in order of priority. Give a deadline for the action plan to be delivered to you.

- ■ Budget the blitz team. Remember what I said about budgeting in Chapter 11? If it isn't in the budget, it isn't.

- ■ Ask the blitz team to report to you with a straightforward word-of-mouth marketing action plan in the form of SMART objectives (Specific, Measurable, Attainable, Relevant, Time-bound). Insist they use the action planner format I've included under the "Tools" section of this chapter. Why? Because the format is simple and effective.

- ■ Give your team the proper tools to do the job, turn your people loose, and get out of the way.

When I took on the leadership of IAWA, my own blitz team—although I hadn't coined such a term back then—consisted of four members of the association staff. The first thing I did for the team was to establish "Operation Zero." I told them that nothing that had been done "the way we've always done it" was worth a plugged nickel. Further, nothing we planned to do in the future could be done with the expectation of any success at all. We brainstormed our problems and laid dozens of courses of activities out that we might try. "Operation Zero" had the effect of releasing the blitz team from any ties to the past methods that had failed. Further, nothing that would be attempted, no matter how outlandish, would be evaluated as a failure, no matter how poorly it pulled members or how much money it lost. Sure, the conventional wisdom says never to set low expectations—that's all you'll probably achieve. We went against the conventional wisdom and found that any success, however small, was indeed a success.

The Tools for a Word-of-Mouth Marketing Blitz Team

TOOL NUMBER ONE—THE WORD-OF-MOUTH MARKETING ACTION PLANNER

In the previous chapter, you read about how to get things done. Now I'm going to introduce you to a simple tool that organizes and guides actions toward the result of "done deeds." It's a tool that simplifies enormous tasks. When you use it, you cannot help but reduce the biggest job to its simplest elements.

The mission statements you give your blitz team are a large part of your vision. Where do you start? Start by turning the mission statement into concrete objectives. Let's say your company is involved in family health issues. To broaden awareness of your existence, you decide to use a word-of-mouth marketing blitz. The central part of that blitz will be a family health handbook. Your mission statement: to make our organization a household word in our community this year by using the Family Health Handbook.

That's a great start. Right away a half dozen objectives should leap out of that mission statement. Take the most obvious one your blitz team will have to consider—write the handbook. Let's look at how you can go about accomplishing that objective.

Writing SMART Objectives

A few *musts*. It sounds obvious, but I'll tell you anyhow—you *must* write down your objectives—the simple act of putting them in print makes them a step closer to reality. You *must* list specific activities or tasks. When you write an activity, you *must* assign responsibility for each action, and every member of the blitz team *must* be involved. You *must* set due dates or deadlines, and you *must* follow up and communicate overall results to the team.

Thanks to Bob Greathouse, I have just the device for getting all those things done. I call it my word-of-mouth marketing action planner, which we developed in my office and use in every action plan, including those I arrive at in consultation with my clients. It works!

Figure 13 shows how the form looks.

We'll use the action planner in formulating an objective for "Write the handbook." As you can see in Figure 12, the acronym SMART stands for . . .

Specific
Measurable
Attainable
Relevant
Time bound

Each time you write an objective, you should test against these criteria. In fact, just for the practice, try these objective statements out against the criteria by checking each off when it applies.

1. To write the handbook.

    S__ M__ A__ R__ T__

Word-of-Mouth Marketing Action Planner Page __ of __	Person Tasked	Timetable				Notes
		Start		Finish		
		Esti-mated	Actual	Esti-mated	Actual	
Objective:						
Specific Measurable Attainable Relevant Time Bound **To contact everybody on our list of champions by Jan 1, 1990, about our new product, to enlist help in spreading the word by Jan 30.**						
Refine List of Champions						
Add latest names to list						
President to review list and delete names, if necessary						
Define what we have done or can do for each						
Define type of help needed from each						

Figure 13

2. To finish writing the handbook by the end of the month.

   S___M___A___R___T___

3. To write a 128-page family health handbook manuscript that's ready for the printer by January 15 of next year.

   S___M___A___R___T___

You get the idea, right? Number 3 meets all the criteria, whereas the first two probably don't. A couple of considerations went into the timetable. You start the timetable at the date where you want the handbook in the hands of the people who are supposed to get it. Then you block off the necessary time to distribute, to receive and handle, to bind, to print, to proof, to set up for printing—all the factors that must be considered in other objectives. That's how you arrive at the date for delivery of the manuscript. Now that you've written in the objective, it's time to break it down into activities or tasks. I prefer tasks because the word *activities* implies things to be done, while the term *tasks* carries the additional implication that somebody will be assigned to do them.

Assign responsibility using the "Person Tasked" column. Fill in the estimated start and finish times. You can use the actual start and finish times as a guide for continual follow-up. Throw the worksheet away and use the action planner.

In the IAWA example I've been using, this is the one tool that I wish now I had had then. Back then, I used laundry lists of "To-do's" that covered a 90-day calendar. Each member of the blitz team was given a segment of that list to complete, and we muddled through our tasks. The action planner I use now is indispensable for such undertakings because it is simple and systematic.

This action planner tool is effective, and once you use it with a word-of-mouth marketing blitz team, you'll probably adapt it to other activities in your organization because it's a strategic action planner, with the emphasis on *action*. However, you should be aware of a few DOs and DON'Ts.

- **Don't allow a meticulous action plan to become an end in itself.** A hammer is not a tool you bronze and hang on the wall in a display case. A hammer is something you whack nails with when you're building and yank nails with when you're taking things apart. Insist that your blitz team use the word-of-mouth marketing action planner to whack and yank. The pages should become dog-eared and smudged, with pencil writing in the margins as the plan is adjusted to changing circumstances.

- **Don't write action steps for things you know will not get done.** Accept natural tendencies. Certain things simply will not happen. You know what they are. Get the stars out of your eyes before you write an action plan.

- **Do change the action steps as new facts are learned.** Be prepared to add and take out steps as you move through the process.

- **Do adjust your dates to allow for flexibility.**

- **Do manage the critical few—avoid the many.** As we discussed in the previous chapter, in the section on "What gets measured gets done," stick to business. Don't let the blitz team try to do everything, only the really important things. You know as well as I do that there are people in this world who can analyze like crazy. In-depth analysis is a valuable activity, but remember, this is an *action* planner, with the emphasis on *action*.

■ **Do use your best people on the blitz team.** Even if you have to take your best people away from other jobs, do it. Your commitment to succeeding with the word-of-mouth marketing blitz depends on your commitment to excellence in the people who prepare and execute the action planner.

■ **Do take time to celebrate your successes as they occur.** Success breeds success, so celebrate when intermediate tasks and objectives are accomplished. Don't wait for the end of the mission.

■ **Do use incentives.** Make rewards an integral part of your follow-up as the process goes along. In that way, you'll not just be the person looking over everybody else's shoulder. You will have control, and your blitz team will enjoy the motivation.

■ **Do stay focused.** Make sure the objectives in the action planners are all aimed at accomplishing the mission. Then make sure everybody adheres to the action planners, no matter how many adjustments are made.

■ **Do ask for help.** Don't be afraid to get help from your subordinates, superiors and peers when things go wrong. It's foolish to let your ego keep you from being the best.

Tool Number Two—The Word-of-Mouth Marketing Pyramid

Remember the word-of-mouth marketing pyramid? You were introduced to it in Chapter 4. Let me refresh your memory about it. Briefly, the pyramid is a new way of looking at what you call the *customer*. That term is inadequate to describe the people you do business with and people you want to attract to your business. Actually, there are five different levels of customers. Each level is defined differently. Each has different needs. Each is capable of benefiting your business in different ways with different limitations. You must employ different strategies with each level in order to become effective with your word-of-mouth marketing blitz.

These five levels include:

- **Suspect**
- **Prospect**
- **Customer**
- **Client**
- **Champion**

What makes the word-of-mouth marketing pyramid so descriptive is the idea that in climbing the pyramid, you find a progression from the largest group at the bottom to the least numerous group, champions, at the top. You also find a closer, more sophisticated relationship as you climb the pyramid and deal with higher levels.

Most important of all in using this pyramid is the idea that legendary businesses use word-of-mouth marketing strategies to move everybody on one level up to higher levels. The higher up the pyramid, the more influential are the members of the segment.

The word-of-mouth marketing pyramid as I've described it becomes part of the blueprint for identifying your market segments, targets, public, audiences, or whatever you call the people you want to reach. Here are some tips for using that blueprint:

Develop a Pyramid Within Each Market Segment

For instance, suppose you're president of a parent-teachers organization (PTO) at your elementary school. The PTO plans to raise funds for playground equipment using a carnival theme. You would identify the segments who might contribute to the word-of-mouth campaign as school board, school faculty, PTO membership, parents at large, your school's children, the student population of other schools, community businesses, the media, and so on. Many marketing efforts would stop there, but not yours. A separate word-of-mouth marketing pyramid is imposed on every group and each segment of the pyramid is identified, by name, if possible.

Single Out the Most Powerful Players

These are the champions at the top of the pyramid in each market segment. If you can motivate and influence them, they in turn will influence many others. Obviously, it pays to devote the majority of your resources to the the most powerful segment on your pyramid.

Regis McKenna, in *The Regis Touch*, says the targets for a word-of-mouth campaign fall into several categories: the financial community, industry-watchers, the press, the selling chain, and the community. He also includes customers. I emphasize the champions among the entire population of customers.

Tom Peters, in *Thriving on Chaos*, recommends asking four key questions in a word-of-mouth marketing blitz: Am I devoting 75 percent of my marketing effort—dollars and energy—to activating a word-of-mouth network? Are all of my salespersons devoting a specific—and sizable—share of time (and money) to user network development and expansion? Are they compensated for doing so? Is every employee a conscientious network developer among his or her colleagues?

"Based upon the answers," Peters says, "develop a sixty-day word-of-mouth blitz (targeted very precisely on a few key progressive customers) to re-launch or enhance product/service acceptance."

Henry Rosso, of San Rafael, California, is considered by many to be the guru of ethical fund raising in nonprofit organizations. He says, "Fund raising is based on knowing the facts, taking time to find out about the marketplace—Great Falls, Montana, is very different from Hannibal, Missouri—what works in one place won't work in the other."

Rosso is one of the founders of The Fund Raising School, now an integral part of Indiana University's Center for Philanthropy. According to Rosso's teachings, fund raisers must examine their target donors with the superimposed figure of—you guessed it—a pyramid.

At the top of that pyramid are the most powerful donors. "The top gift in a capital campaign must be 10 percent of the whole," Rosso says. Altogether, he adds, 10 percent of the donors account for 90 percent of all contributions. The remainder comes from the entire rest of the campaign.

Let's plug in some numbers to see how that percentage pyramid works. Suppose $1 million is needed to stock the bookshelves in a new wing of the library for your university. One way to obtain the money would be to seek a million donors and ask for a dollar from each. It's impossible to raise money effectively that way, Rosso says, because the cost of soliciting that many people would be prohibitive—not to mention the logistics of finding a million people who would care enough about a single university to donate money.

It is far better to identify a much smaller potential donor group. Among those people, you would seek at least one donor who would contribute $100,000, a kind of super-champion. Three others would be required to donate $50,000, and eight would be expected to give $25,000. At this rate, 12 gifts would amount to $450,000 at the champion level. The next 117 donors would have to give gifts of $10,000 from 12 people, $5,000 from 25 people, and $2,500 from 80 people, totalling another $450,000. The remaining $100,000 would come from remaining gifts of various smaller sizes. Rosso suggests that ratios like these virtually dictate the planning for campaigns in not-for-profit organizations. In other words, if you can't identify a large enough universe to find 129 people capable of giving and willing to give at the levels indicated, the campaign might as well be scrapped.

In this fund raising example, you will find principles with clear parallels to the word-of-mouth marketing pyramid, and many lessons to learn. For instance, if your population did not include the super-champion and 128 others to give the bulk of the required amount, the campaign will have to be abandoned altogether, or the population will have to be expanded. In a word-of-mouth marketing blitz, the lack of champions who can make a difference might mean you would have to spend a much greater proportion of your total resources to reach the same networks that a champion can reach with little effort.

When I took over the IAWA, I quickly learned, using my tried and proven method of doing things the hard way the first time, that I couldn't travel the state to recruit members personally. By the time I made my run through the southern half of Indiana and headed north for a few weeks, I'd lost as many members in the south as I'd gained in the north, so I went looking for champions. I found manufacturers sales representatives who called on potential members every day. I found an insurance group that specialized in automotive businesses, and its representatives called on everybody I wanted to visit but would never be able to. There were potential champions among business forms representatives and boosters even among my own board. I started converting these people to being my champions, and they helped me build membership in the association. Together we cooperated on insurance and service programs and regional shows that benefited the manufacturers, the insurance group, and, of course, the membership of my association. I was amazed at how simple my job became after I had champions in my corner.

When I wanted to generate a word-of-mouth campaign about my book, *How To Grow Your Auto Parts Business*, I began by making lists. The first and most important list contained all those companies and associations with whom I had developed sound business relationships and advocates who could be called champions. I sent an autographed copy of the book to each one to show my appreciation for our relationship. I followed up with more letters and telephone calls to reinforce the relationship and to find out how well the book was received by them. Finally, I asked for their help in spreading the word about the book. From among these champions came bulk buys of the book, offers to run news items and ad flyers in an association newsletter, book reviews in trade publications, and testimonials to use in my own advertising campaign.

Identify Your Champions' Essential Networks

When the champions start talking, you will want to know what kinds of people they will be reaching. Using the first list for my book, I drew a series of vertical lines on the page to make columns. In the first column, I identified the networks to which my champions had access. In some cases, these were publishers with major magazines and newspapers. In other cases, the champions were owners of major parts store chains. In still others, the owners were single-store operations with smaller networks.

Identify Ways Your Champions Can Help You

With my book, I obviously wanted to know if the editors and publishers liked the content. If so, I wanted a favorable review. I wanted other champions to buy books as guides for managers and employees or as gifts to customers. From still other champions, I asked for testimonials I could use in my own promotions. Using a second column on the list, I identified all the ways my champions could help with the word-of-mouth campaign.

Make It Easy for Champions To Help You

When I asked for reviews for my book, I included a summary of the contents and an outline of the most important areas for each editor. When state automotive associations agreed to offer the book to their memberships, I provided a customized flyer to each association. Remember, your champions may help you out of the goodness of their hearts, but they'll help you more quickly if you can make it easy for them to do so.

Reward Your Champions

Unbalance the word-of-mouth marketing budget in favor of groups at the top of the pyramid. You might send a brochure in a direct mailing campaign to a cold list. But to the Champion, you will want to send a brochure, a personal note, and a box of chocolates. Do you get the idea? Spend more money on your champions. Remember, your strong relationship with a champion is, after all, a *business* relationship. There should be some form of business reward to those who help you. These can be direct "tit-for-tat" payoffs, such as I used in the profit sharing on sales of books by associations. For other champions, the payoff was not so immediate, but I never forgot them. Whenever I have the chance to mention one of my champions in an article as an example of excellent management, I do so. Every chance I get to refer business to them, I do.

TOOL NUMBER THREE—THE ASK PRINCIPLE

This blitz team tool should really be titled, "Research Tools." Although I will give you a number of research tools, the primary one I emphasize is asking. Remember the twelfth rule of word-of-mouth marketing. Keep the blitz team's research simple—teach them to ask for the information and tools to get the job done.

Use the "Ask Principle" to solicit ideas within the company and from your champions. Ask your clients and your customers. Ask for ways they can help you and ways you can help them. This technique gets them involved and generates many fresh ideas, as the champions virtually become blitz team members. Asking is an art in itself, a form of research that ought to be more formalized in more businesses.

In my campaign to turn around the IAWA, the ask principle became the most important tool of all. I interviewed nearly a hundred former members who had dropped out in the past two years. They told me how they had been offended by the association. They informed me of things the association ought to be doing but wasn't. I heard about past promises that had not been fulfilled. I heard about other associations doing much better jobs. I also heard a ton of fresh ideas, ideas that held the promise of bringing these members back. This tool is so powerful, I attribute to it most of the credit for bringing in most of the money and membership in programs begun under my blitz. In all, after this year-long drive launched in a 90-day blitz, the association had more new members and more income in that year than in the previous ten.

How about you? Are you using the ask principle? If you're dead serious about making word-of-mouth marketing work for you, then asking must become part of your daily regimen. It should become a standard business practice, and it must be part of the blitz team research activity.

Consider this—Edwin Colodny, President of the USAIR Group, a fast-growing and highly successful air carrier, is so intent on asking, he goes to the extreme of hiring folks to examine garbage! That's right, garbage. The job even has a name, "Garbology Review."

Colodny wants to know what people think about the meals served on his airlines. Naturally, he asks, "Did you enjoy your in-flight meal?" Then the "Garbology Review" confirms the answers. He knows that if everyone licks his plate clean after a hot roast beef meal, then he can serve even more roast. If the garbage is full of pita sandwiches, it's time to drop that item from the menu. Colodny knows he must ask, ask, ask in creative ways to get the information he needs to insure that people say good things about his in-flight meals.

Walker Research, of Indianapolis, Indiana, has reorganized in the last few years, adding a division called Customer Satisfaction Measurements. The division offers consultation, performance tracking, and analysis to companies that want to know how to ask their customers how well the companies are performing with their products and services. In a Walker white paper, Sheree Marr and Jeffrey W. Marr write: "Organizations achieve a strong quality reputation when they meet or exceed customer expectations. Quality is conformance to customer expectations. The customer's definition of quality is the one that counts.

"When management agrees that they have to provide good service, and they decide that their customers are the only people who can evaluate this service, the next step is to manage and measure organizational performance with a well-designed service measurement program."

Marr and Marr give some basic principles for designing a measurement program that asks the right questions. The blitz team must have a formal or informal asking program in place before expending enormous resources elsewhere. The principles for asking about customer satisfaction include:

- Plan to track customer satisfaction from the beginning of the blitz to the end, but also identify company strengths and weaknesses.

- Use random samples of both new and long-term customers, or, to use my terms, ask your customers, clients, and champions.

- Design a program that can be used monthly, quarterly, or semiannually, even after the blitz has been completed. This ties in nicely with the idea that "what gets measured gets done."

- Use telephone surveys. They're quicker, and randomness is more controllable.

- Ask about a customer's intention to buy again from you and about a willingness to recommend your product or service via word of mouth. Here you will begin measuring the power of word of mouth.

- Ask about all your products and services, not just the element that is being featured in the blitz. You're trying to find out just what elements determine customer satisfaction and the buying behavior of your customers.

- Find out why people buy from you. This means you must not only ask the customer what is important about your product and service, you must ask why they bought.

- Ask about problems in your products and services. This ties in with soliciting complaints.

- *Take action!* Refresh your memory on the section about what gets done in Chapter 11. No research is worth the paper it's printed on unless somebody does something to translate words and numbers into usable results.

"Trying to deal with people without knowing their needs is like trying to learn target shooting while wearing a blindfold," says Bob Levoy, president of Professional Practice Consultants, of Great Neck, New York. Levoy consults with professional groups, doctors, lawyers, accountants, financial planners, and so on, men and women whose practice growth depends on word of mouth.

Want to find out what people need or want? Levoy says, "The obvious answer is to ask. It's so simple, direct, and basic, it's a wonder it's so often overlooked."

Levoy says a simple questionnaire is common. I know you're familiar with those cards you find in hotel rooms and on restaurant tables asking about the quality of the service. Levoy cautions that those cards and simple questionnaires often can be misleading because "those who fill them out tend to be people who either love or hate you."

He recommends the more reliable technique of one-on-one interviews to probe into problem areas and to uncover the feelings of those whose emotions fall between either love or hate.

Very often when I'm puzzled about why a direct mail piece isn't getting the responses I want, I conduct a "phone-a-thon." I sit down with the mailing list and a handful of pertinent questions. I select a number of names on the list and spend an hour or two making calls. I ask questions. I take notes. I never fail to learn from this exercise in asking.

I borrow from my friend, colleague and mentor, M. R. "Kop" Kopmeyer, in adapting the following essay on the art of asking from his wonderful book, *How To Get Whatever You Want.* I asked his permission to use it, and he gave it—just for the asking.

Why Ask?

Asking will produce miracles in your life.

Asking is the secret of getting others to do what you want them to do. Asking will help you to get whatever you want. The teachings of all the great religions are based on the use of asking. The entire medical profession uses this technique to build a patient's history. Educators, business leaders, researchers, scientists, salesmen— all people whose success depends upon obtaining information or cooperation from others—ask.

Ask, ask, and keep asking. I guarantee you will learn tons of information—it's all out there for the asking. If you ask and then act on what you learn, you'll soon have everybody talking about how great your business is. If you don't take action, people will soon quit giving you worthwhile information.

Asking. That's putting word-of-mouth marketing to work for you. Ask your word-of-mouth marketing blitz team to use the ask principle as its primary tool in researching methods for your blitz.

TOOL NUMBER FOUR—CONTROLLED OUTRAGEOUSNESS

Two things will spark a lot of talk about you—goofs and intentional outlandishness. Early in this book, I told you about the Rule of 3-33. Whereas three people will say something positive about your business when you're doing great, as many as 33 will tell a negative story when you goof. It's human nature to love to tell a horror story. There's no point in fighting it. Instead, you can capitalize on that same human inclination to talk a lot by using what I call controlled outrageousness. Use it to fire up your word-of-mouth marketing blitz.

Ever hear of Joe Isuzu? In my dictionary next to the definition of controlled outrageousness is a picture of Joe. His outlandish claims draw attention to the products in his television commercials very effectively.

■ Instruct your blitz team to develop some outrageous ideas to start people talking. Ask them to make a list of all the rules of

marketing—then tell them to find ways to break them crea-
tively. Tell them to research the conventional wisdom for
launching a product—then develop the unconventional exceptions to this wisdom. Fill a folder with "the ways we've always
done things" and then lock that folder up until you have a bigger
file filled with fresh ideas.

- A caution: Avoid the "Pet Rock Syndrome"—outrageousness is
  not an end in itself but a means to draw attention to a superior
  product or service or idea. The Pet Rock was an absurdity that
  sold as an absurdity. You have a great product. First call
  attention to it, then sell its benefits to your potential customers.

Last Words for the Word-of-Mouth Marketing Blitz Team

Of course, you will want to refer to the first two sections of this book to
employ all the possible techniques that will give power to your word-of-
mouth marketing blitz. I've highlighted a few of them:

- **Blow your customers away.** The very last line on the cover of
  Harvey Mackay's (who also wrote *Swim with the Sharks Without Being Eaten Alive*) latest book, *Beware the Naked Man Who
  Offers You His Shirt*, is the line, "Deliver more than you promise." That's good advice. Get everybody on the word-of-mouth
  marketing pyramid raving about your product by exceeding
  every expectation. You make your company and your product
  look good with a good product, but you turn yourself into a
  legendary company when you deliver that product with superlative service. Here's a wrap-up of all the important word-of-
  mouth principles that apply in delivering the goods in your
  blitz.

- **Sell your new product inside your own company.** It's not
  enough just to fire up your sales staff. Educate the entire team,
  from telephone operators to dock workers, about how great the
  product is. When the employees tell positive stories, people

listen to this insider talk. If the employees are misinformed or telling negatives, that story will be passed along as well, and the blitz will not succeed.

■ **Control expectations.** Your advertising campaign must not overstate the benefits or features of the product. It doesn't pay to set up expectations that can't be met. Even in a blitz . . . make that *especially* in a blitz.

■ **Deliver the goods with a distinctive style.** Whatever expectations you have created, exceed them with every customer. Find ways to give bonuses or coupons or rewards that were never even advertised. This will fuel the fires of your word-of-mouth blitz.

■ **Evaluate your progress—seek complaints, measure results, and ask.** While it's essential, it's not enough to handle dissatisfied customers who tell you of their problems. Remember, 96 percent of customers who are unhappy with your goods and services never complain. Worse, 91 percent of those who do not complain take their business elsewhere. A complaint is an obvious clue on ways to improve your product or service. That's why it's so important to listen.

Measurement is merely a matter of establishing a baseline and a unit of measure, then following trends. As a leader, you decide on the critical factors to measure, then make periodic checks. Your most valuable research tool will be the simple act of asking. Ask blitz team members individually about their headaches and successes. Ask customers, clients, and, of course, champions. Review Chapter 10, especially the section titled, "What gets measured gets done."

■ **Follow up.** If you fail to act on information you pick up in your research and evaluation, it's wasted, useless, worthless effort.

It's possible that nothing a leader does or fails to do counts more than the unfailing willingness to follow up. When the boss talks, people listen, but most bosses believe the job is done after the speech is delivered. After the speech, people watch. They're asking, "Is she going to follow up on her threats?" and "Will we really see him make middle managers more responsive to employee complaints?" or "Now that I've gone through the pains of gathering this data and recommending an action, what is the boss going to do about it?" If the boss doesn't follow up, credibility is instantly lost. Failure to follow up is why so few bosses are truly effective leaders. Leaders who follow up—even those who rule like Russian Czars—are respected, even if grudgingly.

If you want to elevate your leadership capacity a notch, start carrying a pocket tape recorder. When you make a speech, even if only to two employees, record it. Listen to it later. If you made a promise or a threat, follow up. If you find you can't or won't keep the promise or enforce the threat, get back to the people who heard it and retract. Make it a habit to deliver. Suddenly, you will find people doing the same for you.

■   **Handle the disasters with blitz tactics.** The corporate disaster demands blitz tactics. Form your team using the best people. Get out front with the top man. Don't try to hide the bad news. My best advice is to buy *When It Hits The Fan*, by Gerald C. Meyers, and read the lessons about word of mouth in the book. You'll see how Johnson & Johnson handled the Tylenol poisonings brilliantly and responsibly, and you'll see by extrapolation why the Exxon *Valdez* oil spill has been multiplied by a textbook example of stoking negative word of mouth. As of this writing, Exxon has spent more than $2 billion in legal and cleanup fees, yet everybody is still livid about its handling of the matter. Within the corporation, from the CEO down, the spill has been minimized, and the attitude has been arrogant. Believe me—it wouldn't have cost Exxon a dime more than $2 billion to do all that it has done, but they could also have fostered the attitude that the company would try to use exceptional measures to inspire positive word of mouth, instead of stonewalling and causing so much distrust.

■   **I repeat—whatever you do, keep it simple.** I've tried to present word-of-mouth marketing as simply as I could. This is not rocket science, ladies and gentlemen. It's common sense focused on action. Good luck with your own word-of-mouth marketing program!

In the next chapter, I'll be telling you about mine.

SUMMARY OF CHAPTER 12

◆ Rule Twelve: Keep your word-of-mouth marketing campaign plan simple but systematic—in short, *streamline everything and orient everything to action!*

◆ Organize a word-of-mouth marketing blitz team with your brightest, most action-oriented people.

- Detach blitz team activities from normal duties.

- Budget the blitz team.

- Give the blitz team the proper tools to do the job, turn them loose, and get out of the way.

◆ The first tool for running a word-of-mouth marketing blitz is an action planner.

- Write SMART objectives.

  Specific

  Measurable

  Attainable

  Relevant

  Time bound

◆ A second tool is the word-of-mouth marketing pyramid.

- Identify the five levels of the pyramid in every market segment.

  Suspect

  Prospect

  Customer

Client

Champion

- Concentrate on getting champions to help you spread the word of mouth.

◆   The third tool is the ask principle, which you should rely on in research during the word-of-mouth marketing blitz.

◆   The fourth tool is controlled outrageousness. Use it wisely, avoiding absurdity for its own sake.

> "Just do it."
>
> —Ad slogan for Nike® athletic shoes

> "Don't just do it. Do it better."
>
> —Ad slogan for ASICS® athletic shoes

13

The Word-of-Mouth Marketing Blitz on Word-of-Mouth Marketing

This chapter is the case study on this book, a real-life scenario of how I used my own principles to market the book about them. It's my way of living up to the saying: "Put up or shut up."

That's street language for the twelfth rule of word-of-mouth marketing, keeping things simple and orienting toward action. The program covered by this chapter is ongoing. Some actions will have been completed before the book's publication. Others will continue for years afterward. I hope to develop many new blitz techniques.

Using Chapter 12 as an outline, I'll review how I used the principles and tools of the word-of-mouth marketing blitz team to launch the marketing program for this book. Then I'll just list some of the ideas, large and small, that we discussed, employed, or even rejected in the blitz.

Identify the Mission

My original mission was to self-publish a book that would expand my speaking and consulting business by lending credibility to the ideas I had researched over the years. This was a reasonable goal. After a year or so of writing, I began to consider the possibility that the book would have mass-market appeal. So the search for a commercial publisher was launched, and the mission changed—to make the book a best seller.

I have raised my sights high in setting this mission for myself. I intend to achieve the highest possible standard. Perhaps circumstances outside my control will combine to hold the book from achieving its mission, but it will not be for lack of my vision.

I recommend you adopt a similar "shoot for the stars" mission as you embark upon your own word-of-mouth marketing journey.

Organize a Word-of-Mouth Marketing Blitz Team

My blitz team included Cindy Elliott, Bob Greathouse, George Spelman, Sue Senff, and all the others I thanked in the beginning of this book. Luckily, I had married the most important player on this team, my wife, Sherrie. She shares my vision, offers encouragement, and imposes certain disciplines on me. I value her opinion, and more than once, she's helped put this project on track. She also put my son, Doug, on a soccer team. What does a soccer team have to do with anything? Doug's zest for sports was fulfilled by a Little League coach named Jack Dickey, Jr., and a Youth Soccer League coach named James V. Smith, Jr. Both men have become good friends and business associates.

Jim is also a novelist whose first books were just being launched when I met him. In addition to being a novelist, he's written for two major metropolitan newspapers, the government, and Fortune 500 companies. Even more important than that, he is capable of organizing masses of information and presenting it in a way that makes it accessible to readers. I had written masses of copy and had collected even larger masses of research. I needed help putting things into order, so Jim and I became the principals on the first-ever word-of-mouth marketing blitz team. Here's how we used the tools of the word-of-mouth marketing blitz.

The Word-of-Mouth Marketing Action Planner

We used a form of this action planner from the very beginning to shape the book's timetable, especially the writing of it. Bob Greathouse, who worked for us as a training consultant, helped us improve upon our format with many of his ideas.

In reviewing one of our very early planners, I find that we set out to establish a number of objectives to support the overall mission of making the book a best seller. Some of these objectives (abbreviated from the SMART format) were as follows:

- Write the book (pretty fundamental)
- Market the book to a publisher (ditto!)
- Develop a new Jerry Wilson seminar based on the book
- Develop a series of articles based on the book, for publication in magazines
- Develop a condensed reading version of the book
- Produce audio cassettes and videotape programs based on the book and seminar

These were the main objectives with which we began nearly two years ago as we formulated our marketing plan. The marketing blitz plan took shape long before the book was ready for publication. In fact, every other one of these objectives was well under way before the book was finished, but we did owe it to ourselves to set a timetable for completion and publication.

Most of our lessons in action planning concerned timetables. Once you account for every activity over which you have control, the timetable goes out the window. Agents and publishers are at the mercy of their own publishing, marketing, production, editing, and other schedules. You must adapt to these schedules.

On the other hand, we were able to exert some influence on the timetables of others by promising to work quickly and in the correct format. For instance, because my computer system is compatible with the publisher's we were able to reduce the normal book production schedule by cutting back on typesetting from hard copy and by making revisions easier. We threw every resource possible at the task of revision, copyediting, and proofreading changes requested or required by the publisher.

In those areas where I have complete control, such as the development of a seminar, the timetable was mine. I delivered my first complete word-of-mouth marketing program, called "The Talk Factor," eight months before the book's publication. This meant we had to schedule the preparation of brochures, workbooks, and selling materials to market the seminar a year prior to publication of the book. There we succeeded in controlling the timetable entirely. I'll discuss the value of this in the word-of-mouth marketing blitz in greater detail later.

In a third area, working on one objective helped make the second possible simultaneously—that is, writing the article series. Because I've written for the trade press in the automotive aftermarket during all of my career in speaking, I already had magazine editors willing to talk to me. I proposed and sold a 12-month series that became the cover story twice during that period. By writing the articles, I was able to make progress on the manuscript of the book. Conversely, by having the partially completed manuscript on hand, I already had the basis for several articles. We found a real bonus in this idea too.

We called the bonus "bite-sized" articles. The original trade magazine articles ran 2,000 to 2,500 words each. Very few periodicals can afford to run such long pieces, so we cut these into a collection of 15 bite-sized pieces running from 750 to 1,000 words and offered them to regional magazines for publication. As of this time, more than a dozen periodicals run the pieces, and we're still marketing them. All our articles are offered with a tag line identifying the material as being excerpted from the book *Word-of-Mouth Marketing*. It's amazing the number of times I've been presenting a seminar and had somebody approach me to compliment me on the articles. It's a real reward to have a word-of-mouth marketing blitz strategy payoff walk up to you and confirm that you're doing the right thing.

One of our original ideas did not work out. The condensed reading version of the book was to have filled in the gap between the book's publication and the first seminar. We reduced that gap by our ability to shorten the production schedule of *Word-of-Mouth Marketing*. The manuscript deadline was February for an intended October release. In publishing, this is fast work—the time between acceptance of a final manuscript (as opposed to the first draft) and publication is usually a year. However, we came up with some excellent alternatives, which I'll discuss.

The Word-of-Mouth Marketing Pyramid

We used this pyramid from the outset. It became one of the tools to use talk long before the final title had been decided.

Our first champion was Jeff Herman, the book's agent. He accepted his role enthusiastically and effectively represented the proposal to John Wiley and Sons, Inc., the book's publishers.

Our next champion, we decided, was the publisher of the Professional and Trade Division of Wiley, Gwenyth Jones. Fortunately for me, Jim had already been through the grind of selling books of fiction. One of his finest contributions to my own sanity was his advice about selling books. The first of his tenets is "it ain't art—it's bidness," so I never got intoxicated by the heady wine of being an author. I focussed on doing what I do best, selling. I learned that you don't sell a book to a reader. First you must sell it to a whole string of people between you and the reader—agent, editor, publisher, publicity department head, marketing department executive, every member of the sales staff, book distributors, booksellers, reviewers, newspaper and magazine editors—and you must sell it so convincingly that each person in that string becomes a champion. That's how you multiply the selling power of your words and ideas long before books ever reach the bookstands. I'll tell you how we "sank our teeth" into this problem under the section about controlled outrageousness.

We decided to make champions out of the following:

- Every client who had ever sponsored one of my seminars
- Every association that had agreed to be a distributor for one of my previous books
- Each company or organization mentioned in the book
- Selected champions already in my word-of-mouth marketing pyramid for consulting and other services
- Every seminar attendee who heard me speak, but most especially those who heard the parts of my word-of-mouth marketing system that had been integrated into a seminar topic
- Selected businesses, associations, and organizations across the country
- Editors and publishers besides those in the publishing, business, and management press, and newspapers who you would expect to review and critique the book. Here we decided to target newsletter editors and house organ publishers.

The Ask Principle

I've asked a truckload of questions from the first day I decided to self-publish the book that became *Word-of-Mouth Marketing*, published by Wiley.

In my research, I've sent questionnaires asking about experiences in dealing with service. In my travels crisscrossing the country, I've asked thousands of questions of other men and women who either dispense service and generate talk, or who receive service and pass along the word of mouth generated. I've interviewed dozens of men and women for the quotations in the book. I've asked business executives and customer service managers to tell me the value of word of mouth. This process does sound as if it precedes the marketing of the book, but by asking, we created an awareness of the concepts of word of mouth. In building a list of people we asked, we also built a list of potential book buyers.

Among the things I asked for and received in the marketing of this book was advertising space in the trade magazines for which I write.

When I began presenting talk factor seminars in early 1990, I used the questionnaires of seminar attendees to continue to gather research. Attendees continue to provide new perspectives on word-of-mouth marketing. I've gotten more than a few fresh secrets to include in this and future editions of the book. Another thing I asked for was advance orders, the names and addresses of people who would buy the book once it was published. If I am standing before a captive audience, sharing the techniques of word-of-mouth marketing, I am selling. I sell the principles, the process, the speaker, and, of course, the book. If I can't make a sale after a two-, four-, or six-hour presentation, I have no business calling myself a salesman. Asking for the sale is the simplest way to close. Now that the book is out, I ask for the order and for payment on the spot.

I also called my champions and clients who received my big hitter bounce-back brochure and package to ask them their impression of it and its usefulness. I learned many ways to adjust my approach to sell the talk factor seminar.

I asked my publisher for some things not usually given to authors. Among the things I asked for was the right to submit ideas for the dust jacket copy. My top three concepts were used as "cover lines" or "bullets." I asked for and received the right to review the copy written for the dust jacket.

I asked for the opportunity to address Wiley's sales and marketing staff at their sales meeting prior to publication, so I could deliver to them some of the tips they could use from the book (in their sales calls to get support for the book from book sellers and distributors). I was not allowed to address the group, but I discussed in full the material that ought to be highlighted in talking to the sales staff.

Controlled Outrageousness

I wanted to build a measure of outrageousness into a talk factor seminar package that I developed in concert with this book. After some research and plain old tossing around of ideas, my blitz team came up with the idea of chattering false teeth. A short search produced one variety of wind-up teeth that hopped around on little feet. Right away, I adopted the idea and tried it out. Using the ask principle, I put those teeth into the hands of dozens of my friends, family, and colleagues and asked for a reaction.

Immediately, I knew I had hit upon something. Every time I set those teeth on a table top or desk, the person would light up and watch the teeth hop and chatter. When the demonstration was over, he or she would grab the teeth, wind them up, and set them to work marketing again.

It was cute. It was gimmicky. It was outrageous.

Now I had to make sure the effect of the teeth was kept under control. After all, a set of wind-up teeth does not a seminar or a book or a word-of-mouth marketing blitz make.

Our blitz team finally decided we could use the teeth by putting a talk factor label on them. The teeth would not be sent except as part of a follow-up or "bounce-back" package to somebody who had already made an inquiry about word-of-mouth marketing in response to a referral, a qualified direct-mail inquiry, or to one of my champions.

The teeth would always accompany a brochure and letter of a more serious nature, and the entire package would be a box with a label on top. The label would say, "Listen . . . what are people saying about you?" When the box was opened, the wound-up teeth would chatter. I'd have the person's attention. Next the teeth would be wound up a second time and would be set free. The teeth would go on a desktop as a conversation piece. The brochure and letter would come out of the box. Most importantly, my printed material would get read. I tested this philosophy dozens and dozens of times with people. I asked people for their reactions to the materials. Nobody failed to connect the teeth to the seminar brochure and program I was marketing.

By themselves, the teeth were outrageous only. With a package, their outrageousness was brought under control. Without that control, you'd have the "Pet Rock Syndrome" I described in Chapter 12.

We confronted a similar situation in discussing the art for the cover of the book. At first I wanted a photograph of many sets of these teeth chattering around on a tabletop. Some would be blurred to show motion, others would just be sitting at rest. Eventually, on the recommendation of our publisher, the idea was shelved for fear of trivializing the importance of the message the book is intended to convey.

Many of the word-of-mouth marketing blitz ideas and strategies we have either used or considered fit into more than one of the categories of tools above. I present them now with a simple explanation. You decide where they should fit. You judge them on their merits.

- **The talk factor logo.** Long before the book cover was to be produced, I needed art to sell the seminars, which in turn would sell the book. I had DesignOgden, owned by my friend and colleague, Craig Ogden, come up with a concept. We use it on our letterhead, brochures, and business cards. Figure 14 is a sample of the logo.

Figure 14

The artwork gets across the idea of talking heads nicely. It was another suggestion we submitted for consideration for cover art. It wasn't accepted, either.

- **The word-of-mouth marketing poster.** This has proved to be a word-of-mouth marketing gem. I pulled the 12 rules of word-of-mouth marketing and the bonus rule from the book and put them onto a poster with the DesignOgden-designed logo. It became part of my marketing package for the seminar. I gave it to seminar attendees. People love checklists, which is what this poster becomes. It gives useful principles. It can jog the memory if you've heard the seminar. It simply demands that you buy the book to fill in the enormous blanks between the rules.

- **The newsletter that wasn't.** I intended to use a word-of-mouth marketing newsletter from the very first. Very late in the game I scrapped the idea because the explosion of desktop publishing has spawned hundreds of newsletters. Most of these fall under the category of junk mail. Instead, I developed . . .

- **The word-of-mouth marketing bulletin.** At first glance, this would seem to be a one-sheet newsletter, but that's not so. This bulletin takes advantage of the newsletter explosion described in the item above. Its purpose is to keep people talking by maintaining a "top of the mind" awareness. By packaging word-of-mouth marketing book excerpts into what I call the "Boxes and Bullets" format, we make the material easy to use. Next, we do not try to sell the material or even mail to potential book buyers. Instead, we send out bulletin to the thousands of newsletter editors that have found themselves with that age-old problem of publishers—the never-ending hunger for copy. In this way, we're able to make champions of newsletter publishers (and newspapers and magazines, too, by the way). They multiply our ability to tell the word-of-mouth marketing story by telling it to their readership in a very palatable form every month.

- **The word-of-mouth marketing news release.** We used the old standard in getting the word out, the news release. We try to package our material in boxes and bullets so it's more tempting to editors. We have had some success in this effort.

- **The word-of-mouth marketing book review.** Thousands of newspapers simply do not have the resources to keep a staff or even a freelancer busy reviewing books, so we wrote our own review, trying to accentuate the positive, of course, but not making the review a blatant sales piece. This saves the editor time. We enclose a copy of the book so the reviewer can toss out our material and write his own. We find ours is used much of the time.

- **Executive guides.** We decided that several sections of the book could stand alone in the form of pamphlets. These are "Writing SMART Objectives," "How to Get Things Done," and the "Five-Breath Method of Defusing Furious Customers." These guides went to selected executives to cultivate champions for word-of-mouth marketing. In the process of helping them do their jobs better, we hoped to introduce the concepts of word-of-mouth marketing.

- **Magazine articles.** Since early 1990 we've been marketing excerpts from the book to business, management, in-flight, and popular magazines.

- **Those word-of-mouth marketing teeth again.** We found early on that the best way to grab attention was to box up those chattering teeth and enclose them with our introductory message. We included them in our magazine article proposals, executive guides, news releases, and word-of-mouth marketing bulletins. Not everybody who saw the teeth agreed to our proposals, but nobody who wound them up and watched them rattle around their desk failed to remember the concept of word-of-mouth marketing.

- **The word-of-mouth marketing calling card award.** I had an enlarged, folding calling card designed. The back of it is shown in Figure 15.

Congratulations!

Your company has just earned a prominent position in the Word-of-Mouth Marketing . . .

❏ **HALL OF FAME**   ❏ **HALL OF SHAME**
The reason for this award is:

_____

_____

_____

Word-of-Mouth Marketing **is the title of a book I wrote to show how performance like yours either generates positive word-of-mouth or causes horror stories to be passed along until your business is damaged.**

You are now eligible to be included as an example in future editions of the book.
Best,

Jerry R. Wilson

Figure 15

I used the card to save myself a lot of frustration. In my travels around the country, instead of ranting or fuming about instances of lousy service, I filled out the card, rating the horrible performance and warning about the negative word-of-mouth marketing consequences. Then I gave it to the offender. In the instances of great service, I passed those along too. I figured the people who had been rude would probably never learn anything and would destroy the cards I gave them, but those who had stimulated positive word of mouth deserved a pat on the back. I expected them to pass the cards along to their bosses. This has proven to be the case. In one instance, a company called Cragans ran a copy of the award in its newsletter.

I find it hard to end this book. In fact, it's impossible—the ongoing word-of-mouth marketing blitz on the book will never be completed. In addition, I wish I could write volumes of checklists for every business to use in its distinctive quest for the foolproof word-of-mouth marketing system. It's impossible, so I'll finish with a few observations.

First, I'll repeat that just putting your claims to superior customer services into an ad campaign will be a waste of money and an enormous drain on your credibility if you don't deliver what you promise in every customer transaction. Remember the airline slogan, "We earn our wings every day"? I've never once met a business traveler who didn't scoff at it.

Second, great customer service alone will generate positive word of mouth, but you can multiply the awesome power of word of mouth by engaging in a systematic word-of-mouth marketing program. You may be able to use all or only some of the components I've outlined in this book, but you must *use* them. Reading them isn't enough. I know of some business that do not spend a nickel on advertising as we know it—they *never* advertise. They get their customers exclusively through word-of-mouth referrals. The dedication to word of mouth even applies to giant businesses. "We're still a word-of-mouth company," said John Sculley, chairman and CEO of Apple Computer, in *INC.* magazine. "Our users are our number one sales force."

Third, even the word-of-mouth marketing blitz is not a one-shot "silver bullet" solution to your problems. You must establish your reputation over time and maintain it every day. Remember, nothing good can happen without a high quality product or service.

Finally, I will end by adding a note of caution. Word-of-mouth marketing, if you've met the prerequisites of quality product and legendary service, is bound to make your business or organization grow. Any number of companies have outstripped their ability to continue delivering legendary service because they've been stunned by sudden growth. You've seen this happen. How many times have you been delighted at the dining experience at a newly opened restaurant, then seen local food critics rave about it, then seen people flock to it as they respond to the word of mouth, and then seen the food quality and service standard plummet? Don't let it happen to you. Remember to limit your growth to the same rate at which you are able to provide the good people to keep generating that positive word of mouth.

Last of all, I offer you a bonus chapter with 100 bonus items you can pick from to use in your own program. Get busy and good luck.

SUMMARY OF CHAPTER 13

- ◆ I identified my mission as the publication of a best-selling book on word-of-mouth marketing principles.
- ◆ I organized a word-of-mouth marketing blitz team.

   The team used the following:
   - The word-of-mouth marketing action planner
   - The word-of-mouth marketing pyramid
   - The ask principle
   - Controlled outrageousness
- ◆ The blitz team considered various marketing strategies to use.

14

100 Little Things To Fire Up Your Word-of-Mouth Marketing Program

This is a bonus chapter. I'll introduce it with . . .

Bonus Rule: Positive word-of-mouth marketing is generated, built, and sustained, *not* on a single gigantic activity, but on a thousand little things done well, day in and day out.

To give you your start on those thousand things you will do today and every day from now on, here are the first 100. Most of them are original, unused, leftover nuggets from my stacks of research material, letters, and so on.

I've organized these tips, tricks, and traps roughly into four sections:

- Internal Operations and Employee Issues
- Customer Issues
- Promotion and Marketing Issues
- Issues of Leadership and Self-Improvement

Internal Operations and Employee Issues

1. **Build a wall of fame.** Hibdon Tire, an Oklahoma chain of retailers, does a lot of things well. One thing is to recognize any employee when a customer writes a complimentary letter for exceptional service naming that employee. The company gives the employee a $25 cash award. Copies of the letter are sent to every store. In every store and at corporate headquarters, framed letters line the walls. In the customer waiting areas are binders filled with such letters. These things are constant reminders to employees of the importance of customer service. Employees not mentioned in these letters try to excel at customer service so they might be so honored, and customers are given the message that they might write a letter of appreciation that will be valued.

2. **And a wall of shame.** Most companies that excel at customer service, use a "wall of fame" that praises employees and good examples of legendary service. In addition, many have added a "wall of shame," which points out examples of bad service that must be avoided. Put this display in a place customers will never see it.

3. **Create heroes within your business.** When people retire or leave on good terms, throw a party, give a gift, or put their

names in lights. This creates good will and positive talk both inside and outside the company.

4. **Install a hotline,** a separate phone line or extension for taking inquiries about:

   ■ Complaints

   ■ Changing orders

   ■ Incomplete packages or shorted orders

   ■ Returns or exchanges or refunds

5. **Ensure you have an after-hours answering machine** that will take inquiries and complaints. Promise to return such calls the morning of the next business day. Promise in writing and in your recorded message. All you have to do is live up to the promise.

6. **Pick up your mail,** which may include complaints you can respond to, at least twice a day. Some companies do it five times a day.

7. **Delegate.** Give enough employees the green light so there will always be somebody around to handle a question "the book" doesn't cover. Train your people to put themselves in the customer's shoes when the unusual request surfaces. Once a decision is made in the customer's favor, live with it instead of second-guessing your employees.

8. **Loosen up your exchange and return policy.** Yes, there's a cost in handling a greater turnover of merchandise, but there's also a considerable increase in the willingness of people to make the purchase—they know they can always bring things back without a hassle. *And, they return to shop again!*

9. **Your employees are VIPs too!** Make sure they have cards with extra discounts. Arrange with local theaters to get company discount tickets, and do the same for professional sports and concert events. You want your people talking about what a great place your business is to work, right?

10. **Use card-playing mystery customers.** Choose a dozen champions, a dozen customers, and a dozen prospects who might participate. Issue them a supply of evaluation cards and ask them to experience your service over a given time. Let them rate that service according to their satisfaction. Pay them for each card submitted. Follow up with interviews when problems crop up or when you want to single out some employee for a reward. This keeps employees sharp at all times, and it generates a network of "talkers." Finally, it reduces anxiety on the occasions these mystery customers do experience problems . . . they now have an outlet for their frustrations. You could expand this idea as soon as you establish its cost and payoff. TWA uses flying inspection teams that report directly to the president.

11. **Get it right *before* the first time.** Ever thought about taking time to examine your product in detail with your customer before they both leave your place of business? Consider doing this if you find an unacceptably high rate of return and exchange on your merchandise. Do you think it's too time-consuming? It isn't any more so than the rigmarole you go through when something comes back. Test your products. Unpack them in the presence of the customer. Inspect. Show the customer all the essential details in the owner's manual. A friend of mine bought a second car with a manual transmission, the first stick shift he'd owned in a decade. It turned out that technology overtook him. The car wouldn't start unless the clutch pedal was depressed to the floorboard. He found this out, not from the salesman, or from the manual, where the item was buried, but from the sad experience of being stranded in panic for an hour on a cross-country drive. Shouldn't he have been told of this innovation before the problem cropped up? I think so.

12. **Beef it up.** That spa retailer I mentioned earlier upgrades certain plumbing components in his hot tubs to give heavy-duty wear. Can you reduce repair calls by such an upgrade to your product? You can do such things with services, too. For my

seminars, I provide camera-ready newsletter items in batches of three, so the associations or corporations can accurately announce me in advance to their audiences. It's self-serving, but it's also enormously helpful. I provide masters of brochures too, with space for the company to put its own information. What does this do? It lubricates the process of word of mouth, by exceeding expectations in a way that blows customers away.

13. **Mind your manners.** Everybody knows this stuff—so why doesn't everybody pay attention to it? Don't let your people chew gum or tobacco. You see it all the time. Why not dispense breath mints to your people, if mouth odor is what they're concerned about? Don't let salespeople chat while customers wait. Customers should get undivided attention *before* they step up.

14. **If you can't tell them why, then why not?** I tried to buy a gallon of paint at the local hardware store. I tried to pay with a credit card. I tried to find out why a $16.95 purchase wouldn't be accepted. Why did the store set a minimum of $20 on credit card purchases? The woman didn't know. I tried to get her to explain a company policy like that. She didn't know why. My choices were to pay with cash, to buy more merchandise to reach a total in compliance with *their* policy, or to leave. I left. If your employees can't explain your policies or make exceptions to customers, you ought to consider opening a bureaucracy instead of a business.

15. **Hustle.** This doesn't mean the scam. Do you want to get customers talking about the way you handled a problem or question? Drop what you're doing and kick in the afterburners to help them out. Don't point toward Nome, Alaska, and say, "Did you try looking over there in aisle 97?" Say, "Let me show you." Lead the way. Get a move on. Working faster is smarter, in word-of-mouth marketing terms.

16. **Take a fresh look at the way you price things.** I very often cling to the old ways of pricing things on the 95 cents or the odd dollars, which is, presumably, more scientific. I think you ought

to sell something once in a while for ten bucks. I also ran across this wisdom from Allan J. Magrath in *Market Smarts*: "In a study of 400 middle-income women, a University of Chicago group found that odd-ball pricing made sense to shoppers on sale items, but even prices connoted high-quality, regular-priced merchandise."

17. **If you're in an R$_x$ business, adopt a bedside manner.** An R$_x$ business is one with a high percentage of contacts from customers with crises. A body shop is an R$_x$ business, as is a plumber. Doctors and dentists, obviously are, but probably only the medical professions have any training in bedside manners—that is, handling the anxiety of the customer before and during the business transaction. Learn to deal with customer fears and unfamiliarity with technical matters first. This is nothing more than simple, concerned human interactions. If you don't know about them, hire somebody to help you. The word of mouth you're spreading might be negative before you ever have the chance to perform your service or sell your product.

18. **Don't go crazy about this planning stuff.** I mean, it's insane that the weather forecasters in my town go through these elaborate predictions about next week's weather, next month's weather, and occasionally next year's. Meanwhile, they seem completely unfazed about being wrong yesterday about today's weather. Military maneuvers only go according to their elaborate plans when the military history books and memoirs are written years after the battle. Have you ever seen a 100-page business plan that was any more accurate than a two-pager? This is not to say planning isn't important. It is to say, "Get real." A good plan will outline ways to make a vision a reality. It will allow a timetable and budget to be roughed out. It will account for pitfalls and variables. Beyond that, don't bet the farm on anybody's inch-thick five-year plan.

19. **Nodding and smiling isn't cheese.** I went to a salad bar lunch and found the cheese cubes frozen and inedible. I pointed it out

to the help and got the smile and the nod, even a polite thank-you. However, I received no action and no cheese. In the first place, this problem of rock-hard cheese was no accident—somebody goofed in not taking out the cheese in time to thaw, then put it out in hopes nobody would notice. That was a bad idea. There's no telling how many people were turned off, yet did not complain. Then the problem wasn't fixed when it was pointed out. When you get caught like this, here's how to turn such a negative word-of-mouth marketing situation around into a neutral situation at the worst, and maybe even into a positive story. First, fix it. Then find the customer who pointed it out. Thank the customer for pointing out the problem and report that it's been fixed, and take him some cheese he can happily gum until he's satisfied.

20. **Make sure every insider knows your products and services.** This is one of the fundamentals you see in every business and management book ever put into print. Why mention it again? Because in half the business transactions you will conduct in any retail situation that goes beyond asking the price of something, people won't know the answers, and most of them won't know where to find the answers. Far too many will be perfectly willing to let the matter drop into a crack in the earth—and if you don't mind, why not drop into the same crack for asking the question? Do you want a niche to differentiate yourself from the competition on the road to excellence, as well as a first word-of-mouth marketing step? Demand that your people know what they're selling—and not just the sales staff.

21. **Use insider headhunters.** If you've got the kind of people you want working for you, ask them to seek new employees the next time you have openings. Tell them you're looking for people as good as they are. You will get some family recommendations here, but I wouldn't worry about nepotism. This is the kind of word of mouth that is usually based on personal pride and loyalty—very few people would stand behind a recommendation they know or suspect would fail.

22. **Let insiders help write the rules.** Stop letting the people in the executive suite drop rules from an ivory tower. Post an outline—in plain language—of proposed rules. Keep these simple. Ask for employee suggestions for additions or improvements or even objections to the rules. You'll get better rules and you'll generate a wholly different kind of word of mouth than from the old way.

23. **Go on a witch hunt.** Again, an insider word-of-mouth marketing technique. Go looking for problems. Ask your employees each to tell you a problem with the product or service you're peddling. The time to ask this is when you're sitting back fat, dumb, and happy, thinking you don't have any problems. The kind of word of mouth you get in response from the internal audience is eventually going to enrich the talk outside your company.

Customer Issues

24. **Pay attention to how you present information to people.** According to consultant Bob Levoy, there are two kinds of people, those who like to read and those who like to listen, although some prefer both. When selling or explaining, you find out by simply asking. Levoy uses words to this effect, "I have an evaluation and a recommendation. Would you like a lengthy explanation or a brief summary? If you like, I could indicate my thoughts on tape and leave it with you."

25. **Use a dipstick now and then.** In a related tip, Levoy says, "When explaining something to a customer or client, after 30 to 45 seconds ask, 'Is this interesting?' People react in one of three ways: Some say, Yes, go on.' Others say, 'Yes, give me a pencil and pad so I can take notes—nobody's ever explained this to me.' And a few will say, 'Not particularly.'" In the third instance, Levoy says, it's time to shut up. In every instance, though, customers and clients will appreciate your consideration in asking.

26. **Don't assume.** Never assume any of the following: the customer can't afford it; won't buy it; doesn't understand the product; won't buy more than one; won't price your competition; won't like you. On the other hand, don't assume that the customer: can afford it; will buy it; does understand the product; will buy more than one; will price your competition; will like you. *Find out by asking.*

27. **Send flowers.** When you take a married employee out of town or demand extra hours, send a gift and a card to the abandoned spouse. Then, once a year, send a note and another gift or a gift certificate to thank the family for being so patient when the spouse has had to put in extra time to make your business a success.

28. **Make it a family day.** Encourage employees to bring in families to see the office or plant one afternoon. Let your people boast about your products and services to the people who care a lot. Follow up with a picnic. What you spend in half a day's down-time will be rewarded many times over by family good will, and, of course, word of mouth.

29. **Talk about the competition.** Post a reward to employees who can bring you a fresh idea that the competitor is using and you aren't. You already have somebody designated to shop the competition, I'm sure, but this method puts every single employee on notice that you value intelligence information. For that matter, you should be paying bounties to your champions for such tidbits. It's one more way people should be giving you valuable forms of word of mouth.

30. **Post complaint instructions in your business** and on your printed materials. Show your customers you will not compromise on customer service. When Quill sends out an order, the package includes a "Pre-Authorized Return Form." This form lists the products and allows a customer to complain by simply checking one or more boxes, for example, "damaged merchandise" or "not as advertised" or even "needed merchandise sooner."

The form also includes a section so the customer can indicate what action the company is expected to take—for example, replace an item, credit the account, or to send a refund. A customer doesn't even have to call to complain. The form is already there. It completely dispenses with the need for a customer to recite or even write down the order number or account number or other necessary but bothersome data. You could add such a device to your invoices as a tear-off or carbon copy or extra ticket. How can people become angry with you when you use such a device, then back up your policy with action? Incidentally, Jack Miller says that his people often get praise mailed back to the company on forms like this.

31. **Don't pull any surprises.** Explain exactly what *all* the hidden costs are. Every time I buy a new car with several hundred dollars of "dealer prep" charges, I bite my tongue and even argue about reducing them. I do this because I have seen new cars roll off the assembly line with hubcaps and other accessories packed into the trunks. It irritates me to find an enormous added charge for washing a car and installing the wheel covers. Tell your customers about every single charge up front, or absorb those charges. Quill explains what F.O.B. is on certain items—in plain language, "You pay the shipping charges." Period. I may not like it, but at least I know what I will be paying and what share the company will assume.

32. **Establish a "Board of Champions"** and other customer advisory panels. Every quarter or so, put up to a dozen of these advisers into a room and allow them to critique every aspect of your business. For the cost of a nice luncheon and a nominal honorarium, this "board of advisers" can give you a different look at yourself. Using the word-of-mouth marketing pyramid, you can select a Board of Champions, another of clients, and separate ones for customers and prospects. You'll not only get fresh insights but you'll also generate a new kind of word of mouth.

33. **Get their names.** Mike Henning, of Henning Family Business Center, writes about staying at a Marriott. "The day I checked out, I turned to go down the hall and there stood the chambermaid. She said, 'Mr. Henning, are you leaving us today?' I said, 'Yes.' She said, 'What a pleasure it was to clean your room because you were such a neat and orderly person.' I was beside myself with amazement. This lady cared enough to know my name. She knew which room I stayed in and what my personal habits were. From that day on, when I call for travel plans, my request is always for Marriott." Need I say more?

34. **Go to bat for your customers.** If your customer has had a problem with merchandise that must go back to the factory for repair or replacement, take care of it. You make the call. You write the letter. You contact the sales representative. It will take a bit of extra time and effort, but it will also start another round of word-of-mouth marketing on your behalf.

35. **Connect** with your customers so you can return their business in some way. I always ask people what kind of work they do and where, then I try to do business with them as a way of returning the pleasure.

36. **Extend your office or business hours** to accommodate your customer's needs rather than your own. I read in *INC.* magazine about a spa retailer that employs part-time repairmen and sets the hours to coincide with the peak times people are at home using their equipment. It isn't during the day! If you're a professional in a field that lends itself to it, set evening or weekend hours. I often ask clients if they wish to meet extra early for breakfast to conduct business. Many of them do. You want to know how to find out—yes, just ask your customers.

37. **Remove the insulation between customers and managers.** Your true leaders will never lose touch with either the employees they supervise or the customers they serve, but sometimes you have to remind people. Set the example. Go to

the front line and talk to your customers—I mean the customers, not the CEO of the customer's company. Insist that your leaders talk to people on customer service lines. Have your VPs handle complaints. I keep thinking of that television commercial where the boss hands out airline tickets so the sales staff can travel to meet face to face with customers. That's not a bad idea.

38.   **Give the dog a bone.** In your business, you may have formed the habit of giving a small treat to children. Adapt that to pets too, if you can. Give away a dog biscuit or a cat treat—after asking the owner's permission, of course.

39.   **Fill the bloody tank!** This is a pet peeve. I hate spending from $10,000 to $30,000 for a new automobile and driving off the lot with the "empty fuel" light blinking. Why can't car dealers just invest the $20 in the small satisfaction it gives a customer? Starting with my last car purchase, I told the salesman in our first contact that if he didn't fill the tank before I drove the car away, I wouldn't buy from him. Can you guess what he did? Are you inflicting nickel and dime irritants on customers who buy big-ticket items? It's a bad idea.

40.   **See it from the little guy's point of view.** Do you want some items you sell to appeal to children? Put them where children can see and touch them. Children are extremely tactile. Get down on your knees. Sit on the floor. Look around with your new viewpoint. That's how a child sees your place of business. In our town, Border's book store has a children's play area in the children's book section.

41.   **Promote your customers to VIPs.** Issue cards to them (you can use your check approval cards). With this VIP status, you can do any number of things. You can place VIPs on special mailing lists to announce restricted sales. The Office Depot Warehouse Store chain guarantees the lowest prices to its VIPs. Any VIP who finds an identical item at a lower price elsewhere shows it to the store, and the price is bettered by 10 percent.

42. **Keep track of who's on first.** Ever been to one of those places where you pull a number from the "please take a number for better service" dispenser? Of course you have. How many times have you then stood back in confidence that you'll get your turn, only to have the counter person step up and ask, "Who's next?" Number disperser or no, it's not the customer's job to keep track of who's next! It's *your* job. Cut this practice out. I know of a barbershop owner in Carmel, Indiana, who keeps track in his head of every customer who comes in, for all eight chairs, even when that customer is waiting for a particular barber. If you can't do that, use the dispenser, even during times of slow traffic.

43. **Send them to the competition.** If you can't fill a customer request, send them to a place you know can meet their needs. Give directions. Let them use your phone to call. Be helpful in every way. Make the phone call yourself to see if the competition stocks the item and find out the price (and, yes, identify yourself). Customers appreciate the selflessness, and they return to do business with somebody who displays such an attitude. Your competition will talk about you too, and perhaps reciprocate the referral. Nothing but positive talk can come of this technique.

44. **Wake up to the graying of America.** If you're not weighing in with marketing to older citizens, you're probably ignoring or offending the gray market. Cater to this segment of the population. Older consumers have more disposable income and prefer luxury items and value-added service. Price discounts sometimes aren't as important as free delivery or reasonably priced installation. Form a board of senior advisers and invite them to critique your operation periodically. Older people have seen the best and worst of most everything in their lives and they prefer the best. Give it to them and you'll reap the benefits of their word of mouth.

45. **Face it, sometimes the customer is *wrong!*** Yes, I know the

two rules: (1) The customer is always right; and (2) When in doubt, see Rule 1. I agree with the rah-rah spirit embodied in such sayings. I try to make every customer happy, just as you do. On the other hand, I accept the truth in the observation that you can't please everybody—or more accurately, some obnoxious people simply refused to be pleased. Here's how I'd handle such a customer. I would deal with the problem as courteously as possible, using the Six-Step method outlined in Chapter 6, never attempting a put-down, and always helping the customer to save face. If the customer insisted on placing blame, fine. I would let the person know I'd like to solve the problem instead of focusing blame. I'd use any courteous method to get the customer to patronize my competition, forever.

46. **Be accessible to the handicapped.** Find out how your physical plant can be made more convenient to the 20 percent of Americans with special needs. Convene a board of advisers on the handicapped. Install a programmatic marketing approach that appeals to the handicapped by telling them of your extra efforts.

47. **Snap them.** Get a camera that delivers quick photographs and take pictures of your customers when they buy a big-ticket item. Give one to the customer and use the other on a bulletin board of champions in your place of business.

48. **Give thanks for promptness.** Every deadbeat gets past-due and pay-up-or-else letters. When did you last thank those who pay you promptly? Do this at least once a year. It's just another way of letting people know you care about them, and it's a chance for them to talk about you.

49. **Break the bad news** instead of hoping the customer doesn't discover it or won't say anything about it or will be surprised. In *How to Win Customers and Keep Them for Life*, Michael LeBouef refers to the auto service department who lets you arrive in a taxi and *then* tells you your car won't be ready until tomorrow. He recommends not worsening a bad situation in this way. He advises you to apologize, offer to make things right, and to give

as much warning as possible so the customer can prepare. This is the kind of approach that leads to positive word of mouth.

50. **Value those who've been with you the longest.** Does a 20-year customer deserve your appreciation more than the guy who just walked into your business for the first time today? Definitely! Let the long-termers know you appreciate them. Give out a 5-, 10-, 20-year plaque, and so on. Name these customers in your newsletter. Let your people know. Take them to lunch. Make the long-term customer a champion.

51. **Forgive them their transgressions now and then.** With your champions, always return the late fee or penalty. When you want to create selected champions, do the same. You want them to know they're in a special category. You also want them to recruit others for that special status they enjoy. Let them know you value their business, that you expect them to talk about you to others. Don't be afraid to call on them to make that important introduction you've been wanting and needing.

52. **Make it easy.** Wal Mart stations an employee inside the door to offer a shopping cart as customers enter the store, so no parent with a child or person with a package has to wrestle with a string of carts seemingly welded together. Other places have a greeter who asks, "Have you ever shopped with us before? Would you like me to explain where to find things or how our special procedures work?" This helps. People like it. People talk.

Promotion and Marketing Issues

53. **Tour them.** Bring people in. Let your people show off your company and products or services. Even dentists do this nowadays, in cooperation with schools and for the purpose of promoting good health. Send people home with something free. The idea of course, is to be great at what you do and to show as many people as possible so they talk.

54.   **Guarantee the quality of your product and services.** Offer a full 90-day guarantee on every product. If your customers aren't satisfied, let them return things. As long as you aren't stupid, you won't go broke, because most people don't cheat. Just make sure that when people do return, you ask those customers to talk to you so you can fix problems with the things you're selling.

55.   **Don't oversell your product.** No tricks, please. Fully and honestly describe your goods so people's expectations are not raised to a level that can't possibly be met. Overselling and overpromising are two sure ways to generate negative talk.

56.   **Brighten somebody's day—every day.** Borrow from entrepreneur Stew Leonard, who grosses $90 million a year from just one grocery store. Leonard's secret is in making a trip to his store the highlight of the customer's day. If ever there are more than two people in the checkout line, somebody steps up and serves cookies and ice cream to the customers to keep them happy while they wait (*USAE Newspaper*, 4341 Montgomery Ave., Bethesda, MD 20814, June 30, 1987).

57.   **Exert special efforts to attract women customers.** These women will spread the word of mouth about you to other women. Start by not repelling them—women hate dirt and offensive smells. Tidy up. Invite a "sniffer" in to detect odors, which very often will keep women away. If yours is a business traditionally in the men's domain, such as auto parts or tire repair, consider offering special classes for women. And— unfortuntely, this is not needless to say because I still see them—take down the girlie pictures. Bring in a dozen women or so to critique your business's appeal. For the cost of a nice lunch and perhaps a small gift, you might learn some things that will improve your appeal to women.

58.   **Men too!** If you think your clientele is strictly women, what about the man shopping for his special woman? Have you taken pains to address his needs when he enters your place of business? Does your staff have instructions on how to elicit

necessary details professionally, so he won't feel dumb or embarrassed? If he's accompanying the woman, is there a place for him to sit while he waits for her to shop? Bring some men in to help you look at your business from a male point of view. For the cost of that lunch, who knows . . . you might be starting a core of champions among these men!

59. **Mine the maternity and mommy-track goldfields**. Every business and profession employs women who take time off to start or continue their families. Often their companies neglect to capitalize on their skills and knowledge when the women are at home. Sometimes, raising a family becomes so fulfilling, a new mother decides to extend her stay at home. Look for such women who can work in the home on flexible hours to do jobs that are driving you crazy because you can't afford a full-timer and can't find part-timers in the field. Use word of mouth to find out where these women are and get the word out.

60. **Work the super champions.** Use the power of the press to help you multiply your power to reach the masses in your word-of-mouth marketing program. You must face reality about your limitations in doing this, however. What you offer has to be *truly* new and inventive—anniversaries and new and improved detergent are ho-hum. You must offer visual proof of it. You can't hard-sell. You must never beg. You can't seem to want publicity too much. Send an interesting outline of your major points and photographs, if you have them. Write the material yourself in straightforward language. Better yet, hire someone with experience in journalism to write your outline. Think in terms of the reporter, who is looking for a good story to publish, something new that will build the old clipping file, even if it's just a tiny nugget.

61. **Don't call to follow up on your proposal**, outline, or anything else, unless you want to ensure being ignored and even insulted. Editors and reporters hate it when you call to follow up on a written piece they've thrown away. For Pete's sake, *don't* call!

They laugh at you and call you unkind names after you hang up—I know this to be a fact. Listen to me—*DON'T CALL!*

62.   **Offer a company newsletter to your customers,** even if it's only a one-page sheet, front and back. In this day of desktop publishing, this is not a difficult undertaking. We used a bulletin in place of a newsletter. You can send such newsletters home when people buy from you or you can mail it, if that works for you. Remember, this is not strictly a sales piece, but a device for adding to the word of mouth by doing something extra for your customers.

63.   **Test out your new products and services.** If you can, place a number of them with experts or champions who will not only give them a true test, but can also influence others with the positive word of mouth that results from your dedication to testing. By the way, even if the equipment is flawed, your bases are covered. First, you can find the things that need fixes before your customers need them. Second, you can refuse to sell the flawed line. Third, your experts will add the footnote about how scrupulous you have been to test and repair before you start making sales.

64.   **Hook up with another business legend** for a joint venture. In *Business Age* (Aug. 89, p. 20), I read about a fast-service florist called 800-Flowers that hooked up with Kellogg's, the breakfast cereal people. Kellogg's ran a promotional advertisement on the back of a cereal package, offering a 25 percent discount on the purchase of a dozen roses. The result was more than 10,000 orders. This is a case of using the word-of-mouth marketing tools of another company to increase your own business word of mouth and profits.

65.   **Do the little things as a matter of policy.** I mentioned this one earlier in the book. It bears repeating. Merchants Tire in Virginia requires employees to find something to repair or adjust each time the contracted work is done on an automobile. A loose bolt is adjusted or a tail lamp is replaced, for free. Then,

when the customer gets a final receipt the cashier points out the "Little Thing." This is a perfect example of understanding the dynamics of word of mouth without having to read a book about it.

66. **Invent your own language.** No, not the entire vocabulary and grammar of a new civilization. Just the new terms that describe unique features of your business. The word-of-mouth marketing pyramid is such a term. Controlled outrageousness is another. People like to talk about unique things as if they're the ones who discovered them. When word of mouth uses the language you invented, you're literally dictating the terms of the conversation. Word of mouth is a term that's existed almost since creation. Word-of-mouth marketing, the term that suggests that word of mouth can be managed, is an exclusive, coined term that combines a common concept with a new approach. I originally settled on *The Talk Factor* as the title for this book, but every time I used the term with somebody, I ended up in a lengthy explanation of what it meant. I have Jeff Herman, my agent, to thank for the existing title. Don't get too technical, acronymical, cute, or far-out. That Volkswagen F-word used to describe car-to-driver compatibility is unpronounceable, isn't it? Fahrvenungen? Obscure, too!

67. **Dust off an old idea. Maybe its time has come again.** I remember my first self-published, self-distributed book. It paid back my investment twenty times over, and is still selling, which was a pleasant surprise. The unpleasant part was that I had intended to use the book to stir up interest in a seminar of the same title, and nothing was happening. A year later, after I'd gone on to new seminar titles, people who had bought the book began asking me when the seminar would be coming along. I printed some promotional materials and mailed them to all my book buyers as well as some other people. You know what happened—otherwise, I wouldn't be bragging about it here. That good idea that flopped last year or last decade might deserve another look in these new times.

68. **Put your bucks behind your winners.** Your word-of-mouth marketing program is going to take shape very quickly, with winning strategies rising to the top and losers falling off the end of the earth. In the early part of the program, start shifting resources to the winners. Let the losers go. If you find out later that those losers really were just slow to mature, you can tackle them again.

69. **Here's a wild idea—enrich somebody's mind instead of his belly.** The Arvinyl division of Arvin Industries in Columbus, Indiana, used to give hams away as Christmas gifts to its champions. Thanks to R. Karl Largent, a marketing vice president who's also a writer, champions each get a shrink-wrapped package of three novels. The Christmas card is from a commissioned work of art. Before, nobody gave Karl much of a response. Now, people constantly call to thank the company for introducing them to authors they hadn't tried on their own.

70. **Write the book on it.** There's magic in it when your company has written the book on the topic you want everybody on your word-of-mouth marketing pyramid to invest in. In this age of desktop publishing, anybody can become an in-house publisher. This book was originally going to be published by my own in-house staff of one, using a Macintosh II, a Laserwriter printer to set type, and Pagemaker software to paginate. In my speaking, training, consulting, and seminar businesses, having a book is invaluable in establishing credibility with heavy-hitter clients. The operation has also been a profit center. Your book will be talked about if done correctly (if done incorrectly, for that matter) and will enrich your word-of-mouth marketing program.

71. **Develop a winning marketing plan.** Something just occurred to me. I've spent this entire book formulating ideas for putting together the pieces for a word-of-mouth marketing program. Maybe you don't have an overall marketing plan, though. I think it's essential that you do. There's a book on the market that will take you through the steps of filling in the blanks as you go. It's *Developing a Winning Marketing Plan,* by William A. Cohen.

72. **Show, don't tell.** This is advice on how to avoid being one of the great idea people mentioned in a previous item. Never call a press conference to tell people what you plan to do. Somebody might come back for a follow-up story on the timetable you promised a year ago. Imagine what the word of mouth on that kind of fiasco might be. Instead, show them what you've done.

73. **Sell the product, not the introduction.** This item, from Hank Seiden, who wrote the classic *Advertising Pure and Simple*, is related to the previous tip. Seiden cites the case of Dr. Pepper, the soft drink that was introduced to the New York market with a commercial that ignored the soft drink in order to talk about the introduction campaign. Naturally, that commercial soon vanished because thirsty people are interested in the drink, not the advertising campaign.

74. **Sell the middle men and women.** Nowhere did this become more evident than in the selling of this book. With my self-published efforts, I simply went to the bottom end of the distribution chain to drum up interest. With this one, I had first to sell my agent, who added worthwhile modifications. I had to sell the publisher, the publisher's editorial board, the marketing and promotion staff, the sales force, the booksellers, the reviewer—all before I had the first chance to put the volume in the hands of the first buying customer. Of course, the lesson is that you simply cannot ignore a strong effort with the people who help you succeed, or they may accidentally or otherwise let you fail.

75. **Be somebody to somebody.** Jeffrey P. Davidson, in *The Marketing Sourcebook for Small Business* (not merely a good book, but a *great* one), says, "A common mistake made by new entries in the professional services field is to try to be all things to all clients, which frequently leads to being not much to anyone... identify the one service or aspect of your background for which you can become known and strategically market that strength to appropriate targets." This is good word-of-mouth marketing advice.

76.   Pay 'em in cash. Enclose half of a crisp dollar bill with surveys and watch the response rate skyrocket. You want to tell people you're interested in hearing from them and rewarding them with cold cash by sending back the other half of the dollar when they respond. This won't be as costly as it sounds. You'll get more responses from smaller, more select lists.

Issues of Leadership and Self-Improvement

77.   Talk kindly and effectively to yourself. You already know you can't get the best out of your people by riding them all the time and by whipping them most of the time, so why do it to yourself? Entire books have been written on the subject. Buy one. I recommend *What to Say When You Talk to Your Self,* by Shad Helmstetter. Instead of saying, "I wish I had more time," Helmstetter recommends, "I am responsible for choosing when, where, and how I spend my time. And I choose to spend my time in a way that creates the greatest benefits in my life."

78.   Visit the real world now and then. Basketball game analyst and former Marquette University basketball coach Al McGuire said, "I think everyone should go to college and get a degree and then spend six months as a bartender and six months as a cab driver. Then they would really be educated." Educate yourself occasionally. Get your managers out of the office and put them in touch with word of mouth at the very front level. By this, I don't mean looking over the shoulders of the loading dock crew. I mean going to places where customers use your product and service and collecting firsthand word of mouth. Don't do this just for an hour. Spend a day or even a week. Get the feel of the place. The Hyatt hotels closed the corporate offices for a day and spread out the staff along the chain to work for a day on the front lines. The company president spent the day as a doorman. You can bet he earned the respect of the people in the trenches.

79. **Follow up on the follow-uppers.** Remember the idea of inspecting what you expect. To do this, you will use supervisors and quality-control people. Then you will expect your company officers to check. Then you need to spot-check these checkers. This is not a sign of mistrust. It is a sign of thoroughness. It is your opportunity to relay the importance of accurate service delivery in your word-of-mouth marketing program.

80. **Spend some time in the crow's nest.** At Atlas Supermarket in Indianapolis, Indiana, there's a kind of crow's nest, a built-up station centrally located near the checkout lanes. The store manager spends a good deal of time up there. If you ever let an expression of confusion or disorientation cross your face while shopping in his store, expect to hear from him. He'll use the intercom to send an employee to you with a command like, "Customer assistance in aisle eight," or he'll come down from his perch to take care of you personally. Now, you might not have asked for help, but he's keenly alert to what's happening in his store. He just *knows* what's going on in his place of business. Do you?

81. **Don't let an accent be the sign of stupidity—*your own!*** People with foreign accents are not stupid because they don't have your facility with English, and they're tired of being treated as if they were stupid. An army friend told me about a Saudi Arabian exchange officer who was so insulted by being treated as if he were stupid by employees of the Fort Rucker, Alabama, Officers Club, he tried to buy the establishment. Any guesses about what he might have done to the employees if he'd been able to? This same friend's father puts on old clothes and a down home manner when he goes out to buy the substantial pickup fleet for his construction business. If the dealership sales staff treat him as if he were stupid because of his southern accent or his appearance, he buys elsewhere. How many of these individuals have gotten away from you?

82. **Listen . . . *listen!*** The International Customer Service

Newsletter reports that customer service communication takes up 70 percent of a professional's day. Of that, 45 percent is devoted to the potential for listening, compared to 30 percent speaking. Are you talking instead of listening?

83. **Land your business in the trade press.** By definition, technical articles published in your trade or association press have more credibility than advertising. Articles, a form of talk, cost less than ads and often go two or more pages. If you want to know the value of a page in your trades, ask the magazine's sales staff for a quotation. Some pages go for as high as $10,000 each. With this figure in mind, you could afford to pay a bonus per page to your employees who get published, or to hire a freelancer.

84. **Write with style.** As an officer or executive, do you pay attention to the way you and your managers "talk" in writing? Does garbage flow from your pen? If so, chances are that everybody in the organization is following the lead, trying to mirror the executive level of management. Worse, if you're writing like a drudge, you're going to be the last to know—you can't detect the habit, and nobody has the courage to tell you. Find a newspaper copyeditor with a reputation for being a curmudgeon and pay him or her for an evaluation—for Pete's sake, don't ask anybody inside your own company, especially public relations people—unless you want to drive them crazy with anxiety. As a fix for stodgy writing, read some titles with snappy writing, such as Iacocca's or Mackay's. Examine William Zinsser's *On Writing Well*. Hire a personal coach. Ask that copyeditor if he or she knows one.

85. **Speak as if you really didn't die yesterday.** Speech is word of mouth. Do people run when they see you coming? You might secretly enjoy the idea that you put the fear of God into them. Maybe it's really the fear you might want to bore them to sleep. Maybe somebody has a tape of your last speech or meeting. Get it evaluated by a professional speaker. Get some training if you get less than an "A." Vow to become the next Lee "that's gonna

change" Iacocca. Ever considered the Dale Carnegie speaking course? It's not a bad idea.

86. **Respect your personal staff.** Ever notice how damaging those "servant memoirs" are to people in power? You don't want your secretaries, drivers, and assistants killing you with negative word of mouth, so don't drive them off by treating them as if they were invisible little people. Greet them every day in a friendly way; it's not their fault if your day is rotten. Keep them informed of your whereabouts; people seeking you will ask them first. Give them a reason when you want something done. Praise them for doing a good job. Don't be so big (small) that you can never say, "I'm sorry" when you inconvenience them or blame them for something they didn't do.

87. **Don't hold meetings, *run* them.** Take control, and keep them moving. Get them finished. Sharpen this skill inside your company, and volunteer to run meetings outside your company. Why? Everybody claims to hate meetings, that's why expectations are so low. Running meetings well inspires positive internal and external word of mouth about the effectiveness of the executive in charge. Follow these eight guidelines. Tell people what is to be accomplished. Insist on conclusions and recommendations, not supporting data that can be handed out. Limit debate to the first item, what is to be accomplished. Force people to be brief. Be brief. Don't let others summarize, do it yourself. Give marching orders. Adjourn.

88. **In a crisis, get out front first.** If you're the boss, don't sit around waiting for something to happen, twiddling your thumbs until the data is collected by your assistants. Those biggest distributors of word of mouth, the press, will regard this as stonewalling. Sending out your vice president of public relations isn't going to work either, no matter how good he or she is. Even the sharpest critic won't expect you to have all the answers at the scene of a disaster. You'll earn respect just by showing you care enough to try to find out the facts firsthand. Ask Lawrence G. Rawls, the CEO of Exxon, about this. Read

When It Hits the Fan, a book about corporate crisis control by Gerald Meyers.

89.   Look for the silver lining in your disasters. In *When It Hits the Fan,* Meyers says seven positive things can result from a crisis, even a word-of-mouth marketing disaster. These are that heroes are born, changes are accelerated, latent problems are faced, people can be changed, new strategies evolve, early warning systems develop (to head off new disasters), and new competitive edges appear. This is a word-of-mouth marketing book, although the mention of the term is rare. If you want to know about the power of word of mouth in crises like Bhopal, Tylenol, Chernobyl, Chrysler, and others, buy this book. Even if you think you don't want to read about those things, buy it anyhow—everybody needs to know how to handle crises.

90.   Call yourself frequently. Ask if you're in. Place an order for a rare part. Act a little rudely. See how people handle you over the telephone. What's the point of a word-of-mouth marketing program that sparkles in face-to-face contact and stinks over the phone? Check this out often. Call every department. Call every level—your telephone pros on the front lines might be top drawer, while your managers and vice presidents are answering the phones by growling their last names at callers.

91.   Surround yourself with no-men, as opposed to yes-men (and women). An anonymous sportswriter once said of St. Louis Blues announcer Dan Kelly: "If he were on the *Titanic,* he'd spend half of his time telling about what great swimmers were on board." For your word-of-mouth marketing program to remain in touch with reality, you need people who will say, "Hey, the ship is sinking," or, "We'd better do something about cleaning up this oil spill."

92.   On second thought, allow yourself a token yes-man. All those no-men and no-women are going to be driving you nuts telling you what an idiot you've been. Go golfing with the yes-man.

93. **Play fair.** I take my cue here from Robert Fulghum, who wrote most of what you need for your own business and personal philosophy in his book, *All I Really Need to Know I Learned in Kindergarten.* Some of his other suggestions: share everything, don't hit people, put things back where you found them, clean up your own mess, don't take things that aren't yours, and say you're sorry when you hurt somebody. There is more. Read the book.

94. **Step out of your comfort zone.** If you want to stretch the quality of your service to make it remarkable, so that it is exceptional enough for customers to remark on it, you'll have to take a few risks. This is not to say that you must walk up to the edge of the cliff and jump off. You simply push at the walls of the box you have built around yourself. Gradually, at your own pace, you will enlarge that comfort zone. It's called *growth*, ladies and gentlemen!

95. **Read the business success stories.** What are Jan Carlzon, Mark McCormack, and Harvey Mackay saying these days? Read their books. Learn what lessons you can apply to your own word-of-mouth marketing program.

96. **Answer a letter with an audio tape.** Send a personal note to say hello, but get the enthusiasm and complexities across using your voice on tape. I can't tell you how many times an audio tape has closed a consulting arrangement for me, but it has been a great way to communicate word of mouth straight from the source.

97. **Accept the natural tendencies.** Draw a circle on the wall and ask 100 people what it is. Most of them will say it's a circle. Some will say it's a ball. One or two perfectionists will point out that it's *almost* a circle. One maverick will say it's graffiti. Your staff PhD will say it's impossible to determine precisely from the data available. People do not think alike, do not see alike, and do not respond alike. If it's a human undertaking, accept that certain things will not happen. You can minimize such tendencies by

continually making corrections, by constantly clarifying your communication methods, and by varying your approach so you reach all the personality types that make up our richly diverse population of employees and consumers. You can also go crazy trying to achieve perfection. Your word-of-mouth marketing program will never be perfect because those beautiful incalculable creations of God—people—are involved.

98.   Accept failure too. It's part of the game when you're taking risks. If you're the type of leader who crucifies people who fail, remember, you might have supervised Edison—in which case, you'd be reading this by candlelight.

99.   Never slaver. You can't let the people you compete with or your clients see your hunger. Once tigers see the hunger or fear, they will toy with you. Sometimes you just have to walk away from a deal you really want rather than humiliate yourself. Herb Cohen, in his "You Can Negotiate Anything" seminars, says you should care about what you're negotiating for, "but not *that* much." I see the benefit of this valuable lesson almost every week. I've done my mail and phone responses to client inquiries, calling repeatedly on a few clients who can't seem to decide on a seminar date. After that I send a note saying, "Thanks for the interest. Sorry I couldn't help." Then I throw away the file and end my frustration. I do get surprises—calls from clients who want to reserve a date on *my* calendar. Wanting too much is a weakness that will become the spark for negative word of mouth.

100.   Do something extra and unexpected. Yes, this item is a repeat of one of the rules you found early in the book. How could I live with myself if I promised 100 items, raised your expectations to only 100, and gave you only 100? Here are some more.

101.   Get a life. You can't spend *all* your energy on this word-of-mouth marketing stuff, can you? Not if you want to stay mentally healthy, you can't. Stop what you're doing. Go out and buy a gift for a loved one. It could be the start of a personal word-of-mouth marketing program.

102. Don't let the battleground of the possible defeat you. To start a war, somebody has to put aside the grand tactical plan, pick up a rifle, and fire that first shot. Have you ever heard of the analyst/researcher who studies the variables and makes what-if projections interminably, but can never recommend a course of action? There are thousands of analysts like this in business. Then there's the company devil's advocate, the no-man who sharpshoots every single thing, coming up with reasons why nothing you do will work. These forms of internal talk can be paralyzing. Then there's the battleground of your own mind. Will this work? Will that? Research is invaluable. It educates you to make the best guess, but you never know what's going to work until you try something. Analysts, sharpshooters, and devil's advocates don't lead—leaders do.

103. Don't forget what business you're in. This goes with the preceding idea. Success sometimes ferments in the minds of the successful, making them forget that people don't want loans from banks and credit unions. They want money quick and painlessly to acquire something they want more than the money. People don't want lawnmowers. They want great manicured lawns with little effort, or none at all, if your product could manage it. They don't want brake jobs on their cars. They want the squeal to go away, and they want their car to stop before it runs into the garbage truck. Remember that—they will.

104. If you can't get excited about it, don't expect anybody else to. Victor Kiam liked the shave so well, he bought the company that made the shaver. He also got a campaign slogan for life. I suggest that if you're not excited about what you're doing or selling, you ought to get out of it. You'll never be extraordinary. Take a couple weeks off and travel. It doesn't matter where you go; it matters what you see. If you pay attention, you see that excellence is always spawned by people who are enthusiastic. Notice any connection here?

105. Play dumb now and then. This is a spinoff of the ask principle.

I saw this tip in *Street Smart Marketing* by Jeff Slutsky. Suppose that you run a restaurant. Get out on the street and ask everybody you see, "I'm new in town—can you tell me a good place to eat at a fair price?" If your competition is named, ask why. Then say, "Ever tried the Greasetrap?" (your joint). The answers you get may rob you of some sleep that first night, but when you awaken, you'll have some fresh insights that will get you started on fixing problems. Ask the local food critics, hotel desk clerks, cab drivers, doorpersons, police officers, and truck drivers.

106. Beware the great idea. Great ideas are often free, but not necessarily the best things in life. There's often an inch or less of difference between a great idea and and a harebrained scheme. These idea people are the type who write to an author and say, "I've this great idea for a book—wanna go halfsies?" In the working world, these idea people try to dump a project in your lap and watch it either fail, go nowhere, or succeed so they can either blame you for screwing up a great idea, rejecting a great idea, or for stealing all the credit from them—all negative word of mouth. One way to put an end to this nonsense is to ask for them to put up or shut up. "Great idea, Henry, let me know how it works out when you test it."

107. Take little bites. Eskimos eat whales, and tiny termites eat mighty houses the same way . . . a bite at a time. The would-be leader lets enormous tasks overwhelm. The leader sorts out the situation, decides what order to use, chops the job into manageable tasks, and takes that first bite. A word-of-mouth marketing program might seem overwhelming to some companies that always knew word of mouth existed but hadn't a clue about how to use it. Take that first bite.

108. Check your course now and then. Are you on the path you started on? Are deviations calculated or accidental? Don't be afraid to adapt to changes.

109. Visualize. This word is different from vision, the noun. Charles Garfield, in *Peak Performers*, calls this process mental rehearsal, or seeing it first in your mind's eye. Close your eyes. Watch yourself presenting that proposal for the company word-of-mouth marketing program. Practice the material aloud. Rehearse mentally. Visualize your successful delivery, the rapt attention, the applause, and the enthusiasm for carrying out the program. Don't be so humble—mentally pat yourself on the back.

110. **Service—the last word in word-of-mouth marketing.** From *Delivering Quality Service* by Valarie A. Zeithaml, A. Parasuraman, and Leonard L. Berry: "In every nook and cranny of the service economy, the leading companies are obsessed with service excellence. They use service to be different; they use service to increase productivity; they use service to earn the customers' loyalty; they use service to fan positive word-of-mouth advertising . . ." Word-of-mouth advertising. Word-of-mouth marketing. Go for it.

Index